OLD BIDEFORD AND DISTRICT

Muriel Goaman was the first woman councillor, Mayor and Alderman in the history of Bideford. She served on the Borough Council for fifteen years until 1964, following a family tradition set up by her grandfather, uncle and father.

In 1970 she was admitted to be an Honorary Freeman of the Borough of Bideford, and was also a Justice for the County of Devon.

Miss Goaman wrote more than forty books, including her Connoisseur Monograph on English Clocks.

In 1983 she graduated with a BA from the Open University.

She died in 1997, aged 88.

OLD BIDEFORD AND DISTRICT

•••

Muriel Goaman

First published in 1968
by EM and AG Cox.
Second Edition (revised) 1970
Third edition (revised) 1978
Fourth edition (revised) 2002
by JF Lockwood.

Printed by Lazarus Press,
Caddsdown Business Park,
Bideford, Devon.

ISBN 1898 546 517

CONTENTS

•••

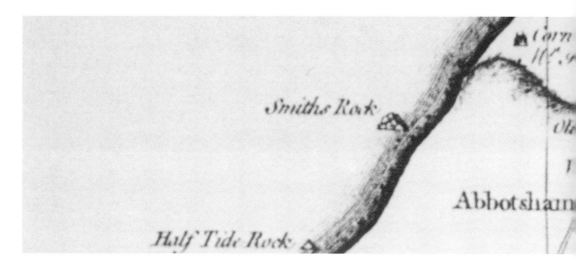

ACKNOWLEDGEMENTS

The author and producer wish to express their gratitude to the many people and organisations who assisted them in obtaining material for this book:

The Mayor, Corporation and Town Clerk of Bideford
The Bideford Bridge Trust
The Clerk to the Northam Urban District Council
The Bideford and North Devon Gazette
The Trustees of the British Museum
The Public Records Office
The Trustees of the National Maritime Museum
The Radio Times Hulton Picture Library
The Devon County Archivist
The Rector of Bideford
The Vicar of Northam
Dr WLD Ravenhill
Mrs MJ Durant, Capt H Jewell and
Messrs J Beara, WR Blackmore, HR Cleaver, A Griffey, AE Hutchings, TR Jenkyn,
LD Knight, RWS Parriss, A Payne-Cook, RH Phillips, MWV Richards, RA Violet and
JHD Wickham, all of Bideford and District.

SOURCE OF ILLUSTRATIONS

J Beara pp 105, 135.

Bideford Borough Library pp 15, 24, 27, 28, 32, 35, 36, 40, 44, 52, 54, 61, 62, 63, 64, 72-81, 84-9, 90-105, 109, 111, 115, 117, 118-21, 123, 124, 126 8, 130-1.

Bideford Parish Church p 67.

WR Blackmore pp 33, 113.

Bridge Trust pp 32, 38, 43.

British Museum pp 26, 71.

HR Cleave, pp 62, 119.

T Fulford p 108.

Golden Hinde Ltd p 68.

J Holmes pp 84, 93, 110, 113-5, 116, 126-8.

AE Hutchings p 93.

TR Jenkyn pp 12, 14.

National Maritime Museum p 92.

Northam Parish Church p 59.,

RWS Parriss pp 46-8, 50-1.

RH Phillips pp 94, 123, 132-3.

Public Records Office p 23.

Radio Times Hulton Picture Library p 106

Dr WLD Ravenhill pp 8-9, 18.

JE Reynolds pp 17, 20, 56, 66, 82, 101.

RA Violet p 129.

FE Whiting pp 30-1.

To my sister Kay Brain,
who loves Bideford and its surroundings so much.

Fourth edition dedicated to the memory of
Andrew Goaman Cox.

AUTHOR'S NOTE

The author's especial thanks are due to the following: Mr LG Firmin, Librarian, and Miss SM Little of the Bideford Free Library, Mrs Joan Holmes of Robert Harper and Daughter, and Mr FE Whiting for their unfailing kindness and help on so many occasions; Mr John E Reynolds for his long hours of patient work in the dark room, and for his skill in photographing old documents and prints; Mr GA Morris of the North Devon Athenaeum, and Mr AC Saunders of Northam for so often helping to hunt down obscure details.

FOREWORD TO THE NEW EDITION

Muriel Goaman's *Old Bideford and District*, regarded by many as being the definitive history of the town, was first published in 1968. Following two reprints and continued public demand the book has been revised and redesigned.

Appearing in its new format, this edition will be welcomed by all who hold this historic town dear to their hearts, and will fascinate readers new to the area.

Old Bideford and District unlocks the secrets of one of Devon's most celebrated ancient ports. From the traces of its early Mesolithic inhabitants, it chronicles bloody battles in the ninth century, the tragic love affair of Britric and Matilda, the swashbuckling adventures of the Elizabethan Sea Dogs, and the cruel punishment of the three Bideford witches. It describes ecclesiastical infighting, craftsmanship and ingenuity, and the work of Bideford's great men and women.

The centuries have seen Bideford in the forefront of British advance and development, with the bold and pioneering spirit that led its sons to the exploration and opening up of America and the extreme north-west of Russia.

The expansion of the town and its continuing prosperity was due to its far-sighted and ambitious entrepreneurs, and there are parallels with the development of the area by the Victorians and the growth of the town at the beginning of the twenty-first century. Bideford's great spirit lives today, and long may it endure.

Gwyneth Cox, Bideford, 2002.

1

•••

PREHISTORIC TIMES AND EARLY HISTORY

A section of the Westward Ho! kitchen
midden showing bones and shells
embedded in peat and blue clay.
The pen-knife shows the scale.

The earliest evidence of human life around North Devon can be found in the submerged forest at Westward Ho! This lies under a layer of peat, covered by several feet of sand. When spring tides coincide with stormy weather, usually in February each year, the sand is swept away by the sea, leaving the submerged forest exposed.

At low tide, when this happens, the remains of a kitchen midden (or shell mound) can be seen. It lies out in the submerged forest, a little to the southwest of the slipway.

kitchen midden

A kitchen midden is a prehistoric mound consisting of shells, bones of animals that have been consumed for food, rough stone implements, and kitchen refuse. The midden at Westward Ho! contains a layer of calcined shells (mussel, cockle, winkle and oyster), embedded in blue clay on a foundation of small pebbles. Burned animal bones have been

found here, split down the sides, showing that the users knew how to extract the bone marrow. There are also hazelnut shells, acorn cups, and flint instruments and flakes, showing clearly the early presence of humans. The whole midden is covered by a layer of peat, which explains why these prehistoric remains can still be found, as organic materials are preserved almost as well in the wet, acid conditions of peat as they are in a completely dry cave.

The Westward Ho! kitchen midden was first noticed in the 1860s, and has been examined by scientists on many occasions. Inkerman Rogers, a celebrated local historian, found oak tree stumps with rootlets still covered with bark, and he concluded that the oaks originally grew where they were found. During the spring of 1904, he unearthed the trunk of an oak eighteen inches in diameter, and twenty-two inches long which, including the branches, must have once measured thirty or forty feet in height. Its top lay towards the land, as if it

Left: part of a tree that once grew in the submerged forest at Westward Ho! The forest is only rarely seen, when the sand is washed away by stormy seas.

Below: the old wreck at Westward Ho! as it was in 1938. It was thought to be of a viking ship, but is more likely to be of a late eighteenth century vessel.

it had fallen in that direction. As Mr Rogers pointed out, the prevailing westerly winds from the Atlantic inhibit the free growth of vegetation in all unprotected positions on the coast, so it can be assumed that this ancient oak forest must have been some distance from the coastline as it was then, thus the land at this spot once stood a great deal higher than it does today, and a subsidence of at least forty feet must have taken place over a large area.

Over the years, Mr Rogers found in the peat the seeds from over a dozen different plants, including dogwood, blackberry and alder; also the bones from seven types of animal, including Celtic short-horn cattle, horse, dog and human.

In 1962 Dr DM Churchill of the University of Melbourne took away a section of the kitchen midden to Cambridge for analysis. He used different methods of dating the remains; comparing the pollen deposit with that of other known related areas, also the radio-carbon method of dating. As a result we are told that the Westward Ho! kitchen midden dates back 6,500 years, to the Middle Stone Age, known as the Mesolithic period.

Danes

Many histories tell the story of the invasion of Cynuit by Hubba the Dane. The earliest is found in the Anglo-Saxon Chronicle for AD 878. The entry for that year reads: "And in the same winter a brother of Ivar and Halfdan was in Wessex in Devon, and there he was slain, and eight hundred men with him and forty men of his retinue; and there the banner which they called the Raven was captured."

This banner had been made for Hubba and for Hungar, his brother, by their two sisters, who "wrought with their needles in an ensign the proportion of a raven." It was said that when the fight was going well, the Raven seemed to fly, but when the battle would be lost, the Raven drooped its wings.

We also learn of the story from Aethelward, writing at the

Kenwith hill-fort, thought to have been invaded by Hubba the Dane.

end of the tenth century. He tells that the Danes besieged Odda, the Ealdorman of Devon, in his castle. More of the details are given by Bishop Asser, in his biography of King Alfred. Asser writes that Hubba and his men sailed from South Wales where they had wintered, "after much slaughter of the Christians", to Devon.

The Danes came to the stronghold of Cynuit, and prepared to besiege it; they believed that there was no water there, and made no attempt to storm the castle, expecting their enemy to surrender for lack of food and water.

"It fell out, however, otherwise, for the Christians, stirred

17

Part of North Devon as Benjamin Donn
of Bideford mapped it in 1765. Donn is
undecided whether to call Kenwith Castle
Kenwith or Henny.

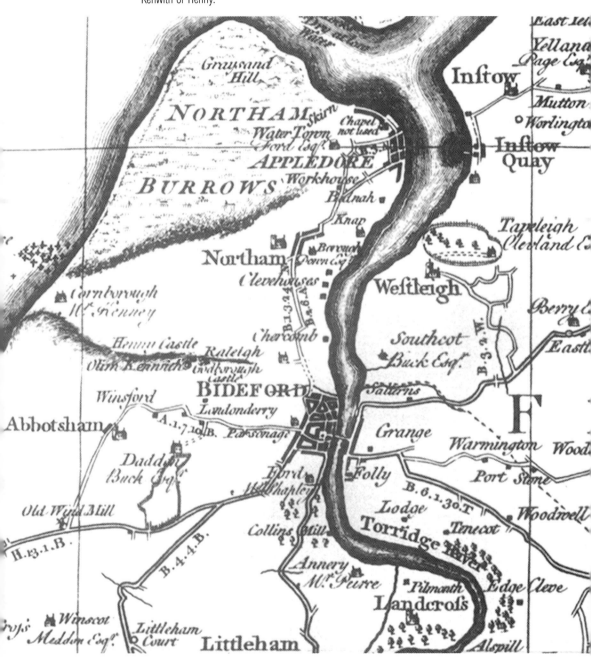

up by God, deemed it better by far to conquer or to die. At dawn, break they out all suddenly, with the dash of a wild boar upon the foemen, and overthrew them utterly. Down went the King, down went his men almost all; and but few there were who got off and fled away to their ships."

So Hubba was slain with 800 of his men; the Raven was captured, and Hubba was buried under a cairn at Hubbastone. The number of men killed varies with the teller, but it is agreed that although the Danes suffered heavy losses, some at least managed to reach their ships.

For countless years many people have believed that Cynuit, where Hubba was defeated, is Kenwith Castle at Abbotsham, near Bideford. This is an ancient earthwork about a mile to the north west of Bideford. Other names given to it are Henny Castle and Henniborough. Tristram Risdon, writing in 1640, said that the Danes laid siege to Kenwith Castle, "which place some have sought for, as it were ants' paths, but found it not, unless the guess 'Hennaborough', a fort not far hence, to be the same."

At Bone Hill, Northam, when excavations were going on many years ago, remains of human bones were found; at Bloody Corner, between Northam and Appledore, coins and human bones were also uncovered. These discoveries lent weight to the story of Hubba at Kenwith Castle.

In 1804 RS Vidal of Cornborough wrote a paper in which he put the case for Kenwith Castle. He claimed that Cynuit was a fort once known as Henni Castle, or Henniborough, and suggested that Henni was a corruption of Kenwith or Kenwic. He argued that historians agreed that Hubba's burial-place was called Hubbaslow or Hubbastow, and that this was in Devon. Vidal went on to say that the nearby Whibblestone, between Northam and Appledore, must be the place for "it is so nearly similar in sound that the most scrupulous etymologist could ask no better after 1,000 years".

Speaking of Bloody Corner, Vidal added, "About two-thirds of the way, in a direct line from Henniborough to Whibblestone, is a spot, which by its name Bloody Corner seems expressly pointed out as the place where this dreadful and conclusive effort was made."

"Thus we have a tradition," he concluded, "which can be traced from the reign of Queen Elizabeth I to today, placing

the site of the original attack at Henniborough and the fiercest stand of the disastrous retreat at Bloody Corner in Northam."

Mr Vidal's paper gave academic "proof" to what had long been a local tradition, and as a direct result the owner of the farm at Henniborough changed its name from Woodtown to Kenwith Castle. At about the same time, Whibblestone became Hubbastone. Mr Vidal's paper was hotly contended by the leading historian WH Stevenson, writing 100 years later. Stevenson says, "We have in this an instructive example of the worthlessness of 'tradition' which is here, as so frequently happens elsewhere, the outcome of the dreams of local antiquaries, whose identifications

become gradually impressed upon the memories of the inhabitants." Strong words, but Stevenson was not alone in refusing
to identify Cynuit with Kenwith. WG Hoskins among others
supports his view, for in his *New Survey of England, Devon*,
he implies that the probable site of Cynuit was on
Countisbury Hill, where there are the remains of a consider-
able earthwork.

The traditional argument against Countisbury is that the
coastline at that spot is extremely rugged, and not a likely spot
for the Danes to land, whereas Appledore was always a strand
village – in other words, the whole of the foreshore was a
hard. Ships could be launched there at all times of the tide.
The Danes' flank would have been defended by a steep hill,
and they had ample fresh water. They could leave their ships
moored to post-holes in the rocks without anchors, ready for
a quick get-away.

Traditionalists also say that when the Danes fled to their
ships from Kenwith, their way led towards Buckleigh, up
Pusehill and along the ridge, with the hill dropping away
down to the sea, along what is now Bay View Road, down
over the hill to Appledore Pool. The first part of their flight
would have been over high, dry ground, with their flank protected. At Bloody Corner the terrain was different; they might
well have met trouble there.

When asked, "How does Bishop Asser's comment that
there was no water at Cynuit fit in with Kenwith, which has
water?" the answer has been that perhaps 1,000 years ago the
stream at Kenwith was a salt-pill, or stream, as so many of the
Torridge tributaries were, and was used as a moat by the
Anglo-Saxons.

Bloody Corner is marked by a stone, put up in 1890 by a
Northam man, Charles Chappell. The details carved on the
pillar are inaccurate, according to the histories, but it is eye-
catching for the tourists: "Stop Stranger Stop, Near this spot

Charles Chappell's stone
commemorating Hubba the Dane at
Bloody Corner.

lies buried King Hubba the Dane Who was slain by King Alfred the Great in a bloody retreat."

In 1946 a young Devonshire girl, coming to live with her grandmother near Bideford, was warned by her never to pass Bloody Corner after dark; if she had to do so, she must take off her shoes and tiptoe past it, barefoot.

Tradition dies hard; but HM Porter, in *Saxon Conquest of Somerset and Devon* (1967) writes: "The theory that Cynuit, Hubba's landing place, was Countisbury seems to be going out of fashion."

feudal society

The Domesday Book of 1086 states that *Bedeford*, in the time of King Edward, paid geld or tax for three hides, a hide being a piece of land sufficient to support a family. This was enough land for twenty-six ploughs, and in the demesne – or land that the Lord of the Manor kept for his own use – there were fourteen serfs, thirty villeins, eight bordars (the lowest form of villein who did menial work in return for his cottage), and twenty-four ploughs. There was also a fishery, which was prosperous enough to render twenty-five shillings in taxes.

In those days *Northam* was about the same size as *Bedeford*, and had land for twenty ploughs. In demesne there were eight serfs, twenty-three villeins, and five bordars with seventeen ploughs. There were two salt-pans rendering ten shillings tax and a fishery rendering thirty pence; fifteen acres of meadow, twenty-four acres of wood, thirty acres of coppice, and fifteen acres of pasture.

It paid twelve pounds a year into the Royal Treasury.

Appledore paid geld for one virgate of land (about thirty acres), which according to the *Domesday Book* was only enough land to support one and a half ploughs, with one serf, two villeins, one bordar, and two acres of meadow. William the Conqueror apparently doubled Appledore's taxes from five shillings to ten shillings per year.

Extracts from the Domesday Book
dealing with Bideford (below) and
Northam (bottom).

In connection with Appledore, the *Domesday Book* makes no mention of a village called Tawmouth, which clearly existed at that time; for in the *Anglo-Saxon Chronicle* for 1068 AD we are told that the sons of King Harold made a foray from Ireland into "Tawmutha", obviously the mouth of the Taw. As with the Danes 200 years earlier, only a few of Harold's men got away to their ships. WG Hoskins suggests that this may have been the battle that took place at Bloody Corner.

Manor of Bideford

For 500 years or more before the Norman Conquest, the Honour or Barony of Gloucester held the Manor of Bideford. It passed down to Britric, whose surname "Snaw" or "Meaw" meant "golden haired and fair of skin". In his youth, Britric was sent as an ambassador to the court of the Count of

Flanders where he met the Count's daughter, Matilda, who afterwards became the wife of William the Conqueror.

Matilda was greatly taken by the blond good looks of the young Saxon, and fell in love with him. Unfortunately, Britric not only failed to return her affection – he never even noticed that she was languishing for him. His high birth and great wealth would have made him an acceptable suitor.

Britric returned to England, and in the meantime William of Normandy, hearing of Matilda's beauty and wealth, "sent deputies by the advice of his peers, to ask her of her father in marriage, who gladly consented and gave her a large portion". Matilda, still dreaming of Britric, refused to marry him.

After seven years of quarrelling, and of actually coming to blows, Matilda accepted William and married him in 1052. When she came to England after the Conquest, she asked William to give her all the lands belonging to Britric, and on obtaining them she immediately stripped Gloucester of its charter and civic rights, and had Britric thrown into prison in Winchester. Here he later died, and was "privately buried".

According to the Domesday Book, the ancestors of these Appledore men were fishermen too. The photograph was taken at the turn of the century.

This story is told in various histories, including *Lives of the Queens of England* by Agnes Strickland, who says about Matilda: "We fear that the first of our Norman Queens must, on this evidence, stand convicted of the crime of wrong and robbery, if not of absolute murder."

When Matilda died in 1083, the Manor of Bideford went back to the crown, and the King later bestowed it on Richard Grandivilla or de Granville. It was to remain in the Granville family for more than 500 years.

In 1272 a Sir Richard de Grenville was granted a Charter by King Henry II, in which

Bideford was given a market, to be held each Monday, and an annual fair to last five days, "on the Vigil and on the feast of St Margaret the Virgin, and for three days following, unless that market and fair should be to the detriment of neighbouring markets and fairs". Bideford was also granted a Town Seal. This Charter was for "the aforesaid Richard and his heirs in perpetuity".

In December 1573, a descendant of the above Grenville, the famous Richard Grenville of the Revenge, obtained a Charter of Incorporation for Bideford, from Elizabeth I, which gave to the town certain civil rights, and in 1610 a new Charter was granted by James I, confirming all those liberties granted by Elizabeth, and adding new civil rights.

This early charter, now in the British Museum, granted Bideford in 1272 the right to hold a market.

During the seventeenth century, the Grenville estates were sold piecemeal, and the Manor of Bideford was bought by the Cleveland family, circa 1750. It would appear that John Cleveland, in 1848 took his duties as Lord of the Manor seriously, for he covered over the market for the first time.

In 1881 the Mayor and Corporation bought the Manor of Bideford from John Cleveland of Tapely. Thus the Aldermen and Councillors became the Lords of the Manor, and they observe the ancient annual ceremony of the Manor Court to this day.

It was not until 1936 that Armorial bearings were granted to Bideford, and registered at the College of Heralds. The town's motto is "Bold for Queen and Faith", an adaptation of

Sir Richard Grenville's dying words: "I have ended my life as a soldier ought to do, fighting for his country, Queen, religion and honour."

The Manor of Northam, which belonged to Britric, was given to the Church of St Stephen in Caen by William the Conqueror, and in 1252 the French Church handed over responsibility for the Manor to one of its subsidiary monasteries, the Priory of Frampton in Dorset. Later it was granted by the Crown to the College of Ottery St Mary, and it changed hands again in 1564, when Queen Elizabeth gave it to the Dean and Canons of Windsor.

Manor of Northam

Appledore from Instow in 1919. The steam-boat on the left was probably used as a tug.

It eventually passed to the Melhuish family; in 1770 William Mclhuish died without issue, having willed that 200 years after his death his estate should revert to the heirs of Thomas Melhuish, Vicar of Witheridge. During these 200 years the Manor was bought and leased to various people, until in 1895 the Royal North Devon Golf Club acquired it, assigning it to trustees to be held for the residue of the said term. The Northam Urban District Council was assigned the Manor in 1962, at the same time granting a lease back to the Club of the sole right of playing golf on the Burrows, which form part of the Manor.

In 1963, Armorial bearings were granted to Northam, registered at the College of Heralds. The motto is: "United we shall conquer".

2

●●●

BIDEFORD
LONG BRIDGE

Horse-buses and carriages
waiting for the London train, about 1900.

B efore the bridge was built, the only way to cross the Torridge other than in a boat was by a ford, where Ford House now stands. From this may have come the town's name, By-the-ford, Byda's ford, Bediforda, Bydeford and other spellings.

Tristram Risdon says that many people using this ford were drowned, owing to the "breadth and roughness" of the river. So the inhabitants "did therefore at divers times, and in sundry places, begin to build a bridge, but no firm foundation being found, their attempts came to no effect".

From various reliable early sources it appears that Sir Richard Gornard or Gurnay, the parish priest of Bideford, built the first bridge. The story goes that he had "a vision in his sleep", in which he was told to set the foundations of the bridge on a rock which he would find rolled down on to the strand. Sir Richard thought that this was just a dream, but the following night he had the vision again. He was so impressed that he went to his Bishop and told him about it. The rock was found, exactly as in his vision, and the bridge was subsequently built there.

Another fable tells that three times Gurney started building the foundations at the fording-place, and three times the stones were washed down the river to the place where the bridge now stands. Supernatural explanations were readily given in those days, and Gurney took this to indicate that he must build the bridge at the new site.

Gurney's Bishop was Peter Quivil of Exeter. He granted indulgences to raise the money for the cost of the work. Quivil was Bishop from 1280-1291, so presumably the first bridge was built between those years. The original structure was of wood, and it had a chapel at each end. We know that this is so because on 7th April 1459 the Pope issued a letter offering indulgences for the repair of the bridge at Bideford, where "there flows a very rapid and dangerous river, in which on account of the faulty structure of the bridge, which is of wood, many persons have been drowned, and that on the said bridge there are two chapels, the one of St. Mary the Virgin and the

Above left: The Church of Allhallows at the west end of the first wooden bridge at Bideford circa 1280 (from a model by FE Whiting).

Below left: This huge timber, part of the first wooden bridge, was found during repairs in 1924. A similar beam was discovered during the repairs of 1968.

Below centre: The first stone bridge built about 1500 (from the model by FE Whiting).

Below right: The Church of St Anne and toll-house at East-the-Water, as it must have looked about 1745 (from the model by FE Whiting).

other of All Saints, which are also in great need of repair."

The river Torridge is a strongly flowing tidal river, and the wooden piers of this bridge must have taken a tremendous buffeting over the 200 years that it stood. Bishop after Bishop of Exeter had to grant indulgences to those of his flock who would contribute to the upkeep of the bridge – there are records of this happening in 1390, 1425, 1437, 1444 and 1500. In 1535 the "wardens and keepers of Bedeford Bridge" were

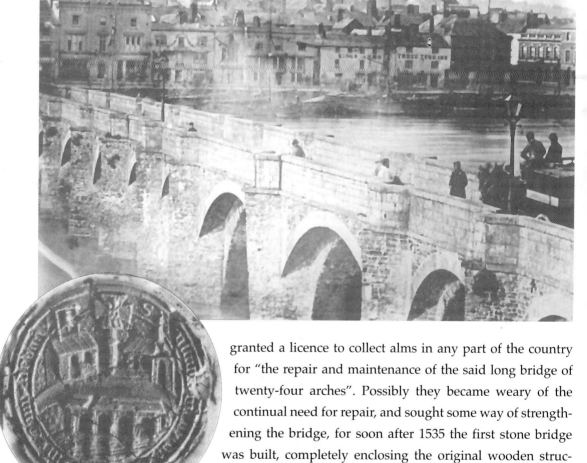

granted a licence to collect alms in any part of the country for "the repair and maintenance of the said long bridge of twenty-four arches". Possibly they became weary of the continual need for repair, and sought some way of strengthening the bridge, for soon after 1535 the first stone bridge was built, completely enclosing the original wooden structure. John Leland, the English antiquary, 1506(?)-1552, writing in his *Itinerary* said, "The Bridge at Bedeforde is a very notable

Worke, and hath XXIIII Arches of Stone, and is fairly waullid on each side".

No two arches of the bridge are the same width, leading to the general assumption that the poorer parishes of the district con-tributed to the smaller arches, and the richer to the wider. The fact was that the stone bridge was built with arches that corresponded to the length of the timbers of the original wooden one. Just before the last widening in 1925, repairs were carried out on some of the cutwaters and piers. During this work remains of the old oak bridge were taken out – mas-sive pieces of timber which proved as the Papal letter of 1459 had already done, that the first bridge had been made of wood.

In 1638 the Bridge was repaired yet again, and this time the parapet walls were raised to four feet five inches. About the year 1692, a sundial in the Renaissance style was built in the centre of the north side of the bridge. An account book belong-ing to the Bridge Trust, dated Christmas 1692, reads: "By sun-dry charges to Erect a pillar sun dyall and other ornaments on the Long Bridge as by pticular acct.s appears to be no . . . £27.00.00."

The sundial obviously proved to be more expensive than was expected, because in 1693 the record shows "By cash to Mr Robert Wren for sundial 10s more than we have pt. for it . . . £00.10.00."

This early stone bridge was very narrow, and although

Main picture: one of the first known pictures of Bideford bridge taken before the widening of 1864 and, above, the bridge with cast iron parapets after it was widened. The bridge was said to be founded on wool, but whether on bags of wool, or on money from the wool trade, has never been established

Left bottom: the Bridge Seal from a document dated 1693. An exquisite example of a seal-cutter's art. It shows the two chapels, and in the centre a Maltese Cross with a relief of the Blessed Virgin and Child. Even the reflections of the cutwaters in the river can be seen.

33

During the widening of 1925 this lorry crashed through the temporary railing. Father and son who were in the cab were practically unhurt.

there were triangular recesses for pedestrians, built out over the piers, Daniel Defoe, the great traveller, wrote in 1724 that carts and wagons used to wait for the tide to go out, and then crossed over the sand rather than risk using the bridge. John Watkins, in *The History of Bideford*, 1792, made the same complaint: "Whether, as the bridge is extremely narrow, the application of its fund to the widening of it (if the design should be found practicable, and the expence sufficiently moderate), would not be a wise and beneficial plan, I leave to the general voice, and the consideration of the Feoffees to determine."

The fund that Watkins mentions had come from the indulgences, and had grown over the years into a large sum. The Feoffees (or trustees) of the bridge had the job of administering the fund as well as having to keep the bridge in good repair.

During 1778 the Feoffees became worried about the stability of the bridge, and on 14th December passed a Minute "that the opinion of some Emminent Counsel be taken on the following question – whether the Feoffees of the Bridge have or have not a right to hinder carriages with Burthens passing over the Long Bridge of Bideford, and that a state of the case be prepared by Mr Lake for that purpose, but not sent away till approved of by the Feoffees." This was followed in 1791 by a Minute ordering that "the Bridge Wardens do in future stop all carriages passing over the Bridge with such weights as they may think will be injurious to the same."

The ever-increasing use of carriages rather than packhorses (for which the Bridge was originally built) continued to be a problem, and on 21st December 1793, a Minute ordered: "That an advertisement be inserted in one of the London, Bristol, Sherborne, and Exeter papers for receiving tenders for widening three arches." This widening took place between 1795 and 1810 making the carriageway nine feet wide and the pavements two feet wide. A toll house at the

end of the bridge and the two chapels were pulled down at some time within the next thirty years.

Frank Whiting, the then Bridge Warden, said in 1948, "The first arches were pointed or Gothic, which was an ecclesiastical form of building and indicated its origin in the Church, while the semi-circular arch was a civic form and indicates that at this date (1810) the bridge and responsibility for it had passed out of the hands of the Church."

In 1835 gas works were built at East-the-Water on land leased from the Bridge; this enabled a gas main to be carried

Right: the carriageway was widened in 1925 to sixteen feet. Evidently the public were allowed to come very close to the work in progress.

under the south side of the bridge, from which five gas lamp standards were erected to light it.

By 1856, the increased traffic over the bridge, due largely to the coming of the railway to Bideford, compelled the Feoffees to appeal to the Charity Commissioners for permission to widen the bridge yet again. This new widening did not take place until 1864-66, when the carriageway became fourteen feet nine inches wide. This was the heyday of cast-iron ornamentation, and the parapet was finished off with a Victorian cast-iron design.

By the end of the nineteenth century, the cutwaters were giving fresh anxiety, and some of them had to be rebuilt. Even while this was going on, talks about the necessity for another widening began. With financial help from the Devon County Council, assisted by the Ministry of Transport, the Bridge Trust embarked on the last and final widening. The work was finished in 1925, giving a sixteen feet carriageway and seven feet pavements. The cast-iron was done away with, and the new parapets were finished in reinforced random stonework, in keeping with the whole structure of the bridge.

In the early days of the bridge, as money and lands were given towards its upkeep, twenty-four Trustees or Feoffees were appointed to look after its affairs. Four extra men were appointed annually to receive the income from the lands, and to see it was used for the repairs of the bridge. Unfortunately, all the bridge records up to 1685 have been lost or destroyed, but this information about the original Bridge Trust comes from proceedings in the Court of Chancery in 1608.

Bridge Feoffees

The inhabitants of Bideford brought a complaint against the then Feoffees, alleging incompetence and dishonesty, and neglect to repair the bridge. As a result of this suit, the whole scheme was put on a proper footing, and the immediate provisions ordered by the Commissioners were:

1. A "perfect survaie" in writing, of all the Bridge and Town lands.

2. A "leager book" for registering this survey, the rents, etc.

3. The restoration of all bridge documents held by the Feoffees. (It was at this that the precious records were probably destroyed by the disgruntled out-going Feoffees.)

4. The annual election of "two Wardens or Receivors and one Assistant by the Maior and Aldermen" etc to look after the Bridge money, and to keep the bridge in repair. The accounts to be publicly examined once a year by the Maior, etc

5. The annual election of two Treasurers to give a "true and just accompt" of all the Bridge and Town money.

6. Twenty pounds to be invested from the Bridge Fund to provide work for the "poore inhabitants" of the town.

7. Eighteen new Feoffees named; and when their numbers fell to six, another twelve to be enfeoffeed. Any Feoffees living out of the parish for more than two years to be asked to resign – "this order to continue for ever".

8. A public survey of the aforesaid lands to be made from time to time. Also, (this being in the seventeenth century, no other easy form of publicity existed) that public notice of lands "to be letten" be given on three consecutive Sundays after Morning Prayer in the Bideford Parish Church, due respect being given to old tenants and local people.

Eleven years later, another complaint was made against the Feoffees, but there seems to be no report of any action being taken as a result of this, and from that time the Feoffees

Below left: the corner of Bridgeland Street with Mill Street about 1900.

Below right: the opposite corner at the same time.

carried out their duties faithfully. Hand in hand with their care of the bridge went their care for the people of the town, and they continually gave financial help to the needy.

The old Bridge books give interesting glimpses of their affairs:

1735	To a new pair of oars for	
	the boat	*4/-*
	To wheat for poor people	*14/3*
	Pd. the Pavor to drink	*2/3*
1736	To cash paid Mr. Talling	
	for Trimming the boat	*11/2d*
14 December	That a dinner be provided	
1778	by Mrs. Chipp on Monday	
	the 21st day of December inst.	
	for thirty persons at one shill-	
	ing and sixpence per head	*£2. 5s*

This was presumably the dinner that followed the checking of the "accompts" carried out annually on St Stephen's Day; on other occasions the dinner was cancelled and the money given to the poor, as on:

"14th December 1784, That no dinner or supper be provided on the 22nd but that the accounts be settled as usual in the afternoon of that day, and a glass of wine and cakes be ordered for the gentlemen who attend, and that the sum of Ten Pounds be given to the poor, under and subject to the direction of the Feofees."

The Feoffees had no hall of their own until 1757; they held their meetings up until then in one of the local inns. In 1881 the Bridge affairs came under a scheme of the Charity Commissioners, and there are now eighteen Feoffees, consisting of Mayor, five members of the Borough Council, and twelve elective members.

Leases on Lives

The Bridge property was originally let on a basis of a lease on two or three "Lives". In the early days, this worked quite well; in a small and close-knit community everyone knew everybody. A man would name two or three young people for the "Lives", and the lease lasted their lifetime. When one died, the payment of a "fine" brought permission to name another "Life". By the end of the nineteenth century, however, complications had occurred in this system. With the opening-up of communications people moved around the country, or emigrated. Sometimes it was impossible to trace

The bottom of Bridge Street in the 1870s. The building on the right with the open arches housed the old Grammar School until 1879.

the "Lives" and no-one knew when a lease fell due, nor, indeed to whom it had been granted. The Charity Commissioners refused to accept leases on this basis, and a system of leasing on "99 years" developed.

Towards the end of the seventeenth century the tobacco trade with Virginia and Maryland brought increasing prosperity to Bideford. Wealthy merchants were attracted to the town, and the time seemed ripe for developing the Bridge Lands, and building more houses. This was the beginning of Bridgeland Street. The Feoffees acquired a couple of small orchards, some gardens, a yard and some tumble-down buildings, all of which they cleared for the site.

In the relevant account books we read: "By one year and a half rent paid to Mr. William Rowe for Crangs house at £6. 0. 0 per annum which we agreed to pay yearly for the conveniency of a passage into the street then intended to be built on the Bridge Lands."

Unlike Bideford's other streets and drangs, Bridgeland Street was to be forty feet wide, and all the houses had to be two stories high, and built in accordance with a detailed specification. The whole street had to be finished within two years of signing the agreement, the architect being Nathaniel Gascoyne.

The Feoffees also built the "New Kay", about 200 feet long, "for the better and more convenient landing of goods for all such merchants as should dwell in the said street." At the time of this development, the Trust's yearly income was £55.1.5, plus any heriots or fines that became payable on the death of a "life".

In all these deliberations it is clear that the Bridge Feoffees worked closely with the Mayor and Corporation, and over the years the bridge became part of the very life of the town.

Grammar School

The Bridge Trust from early times encouraged education in Bideford, and the Grammar School benefited greatly in this way. The earliest recorded Grammar School was on Bridge lands at the end of what is now Allhalland Street, on

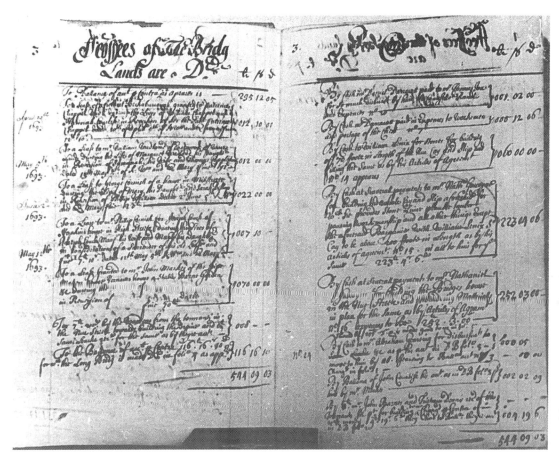

Above: the account book of the Bridge Lands of 1693.

Right: This stone marked an even earlier rebuilding of the school premises.

Richard Dunnyng rented a bake-house from the Feoffees "with the great seller under the School House". The boundaries of this property are delightfully worded in the old record: "Alhalwyn Street on the west, the ponyon end of the bake-house on the east, the land of John Suzanne, gent. on the north, and the Broadway or street leading over the long Bridge on the south."

From this entry it is obvious that a school was already established in 1617, and almost certainly as far back as the sixteenth century. Tradition gives the honour of the founding of the school to Sir Richard Grenville; one of the pointers to this is that although the school stood on Bridge lands, it was entirely surrounded by Grenville land. (The Old Manor

House, where Sir Richard lived, occupied the site of the present Town Hall. The new Manor House which was the home of Sir Bevil Grenville, is situated between the corner of the High Street and the King's Arms on the quay. Sir Richard, as Lord of the Manor, owned the quay and the houses fronting it.) It seems possible that he gave the site to the Feoffees for the purpose of founding a school, during the 1580s.

The school was rebuilt in 1657; the date was inscribed on a stone, which stood in the Allhalland Street premises until 1840. It is now in the Assembly Hall of the present Bideford College building in Abbotsham Road, which was a Grammar School until 1975. There is also here another stone, which commemorates the renovation of the school in 1686, in these words:

> "SCHOLA GRAMMATICA BIDEFORDENSIS"
> *Linguas, ingenium, atque relligionem,*
> *Haec reserat, docet, promovet, atque colit.*
> *This school was rebuilt to ye Glory of God, and*
> *incorragement of good learning by ye order of the*
> *Right worshipfull JOHN DARRACOTT MAYOR*
> *with ye consent of his brethren ye Aldermen and*
> *Capitall Burgesses of this town Ano Dom 1686."*

In 1689, Mrs Susannah Stucley left £200 in her will for the maintenance of the school, provided that the town could raise another £400. This sum and more was readily forthcoming, and the whole amount, £620, was invested in lands in the parish of West Buckland.

One of the most famous early Headmasters was Zachariah Mudge, who remained at the school from 1717 to 1732, leaving to become the Vicar of St Andrew's Church, Plymouth, and later a Prebendary of Exeter Cathedral. The Bridge Trust made Mudge a grant of ten pounds a year (extra to his salary),

and another grant if the number of pupils fell below an agreed level. From the Bridge account books:

"February 28th, 1723. To cash paid Mr. Zachariah Mudge for a deficiency in ye school an agreement of ten pounds due and entered last Christmas £ 10. 0.0."

Zachariah Mudge was the father of Thomas, the renowned horologist, who invented the lever escapement in clocks.

In 1877-1879 new buildings were built in North Down Road, and the Grammar School resumed its work there. The old school in Allhalland Street, having been condemned, was pulled down soon afterwards, making way for the present Bridge Buildings. Extensions to the North Down Road premises from time to time proved inadequate for the increasing numbers of pupils, and after much delay a new school was built in Abbotsham Road in 1935, the Devon County Council having taken the school over in 1928.

The "Writing", "Commercial" or "Mathematical" School

The school was opened by the Feoffees in 1761, next door to the Allhalland Street Grammar School. The Bridge records show: "£10. to the master of the Mathematical School in Bideford for educating gratuitously ten poor boys of the parish, nominated by the Trustees, in navigation to qualify them for the sea-service, such master to have the use and occupation of the school and dwelling-house standing on the Bridge estate, free of rent as theretofore."

Evidently the curriculum widened over the years, for on 26th July, 1771, we read:

"The Feoffees let to Jewell for a term of

7 years a new-built dwelling house next the Bridge Hall, the rent to be one grain of wheat, Jewell to receive 10 poor children, chosen by the Mayor and Corporation, either boys or girls, 6 from the workhouse and 4 from the poorest in the Town, and instruct them in reading, writing, and arithmetic. The Feoffees to pay a salary of £10 a year and keep the premises in repair except Glazing the windows, which Jewell is to do and also to pay the window tax."

In 1837, in a record of the pupils' progress and behaviour, we read of one boy: "Remarks – not to learn navigation". Perhaps he should have been at the Grammar School next door.

George Donn's School

This school, established in the early eighteenth century, was not supported by the Bridge Feoffees but was closely connected with them. The Headmaster was George Donn, who was also the Parish Clerk. In the days of Bideford's expansion in commerce, he realised the need for more up-to-date subjects than the Grammar School could provide, and he taught mathematics, book-keeping, navigation and ship-building. In 1739 he made a detailed survey of the bridge, which was published in the *Gentleman's Magazine* of July 1751, with an article written by his son Benjamin.

A nineteenth century print of the old Grammar School in Allhalland Street, erected in 1686.

Benjamin had been a pupil at the Grammar School, under Zachariah Mudge, and became a brilliant mathematician, and an expert in what was then known as "Natural and Experimental Philosophy". In the *Gentleman's Magazine* in 1755, an article appeared, in answer to a request for information about towns of England, giving details about Bideford. This article was unsigned, but the historian John Watkins attributed it to "my ingenious friend Mr. B. Donne". In 1765, Benjamin Donn's map of the County of Devon was published by the London Society for the Encouragement of Arts, Manufactures and Commerce.

Bideford Bridge has fallen down!

On the many occasions during its 700 years of existence when the bridge has been unable to take the volume of traffic using it, inconvenience must have been caused to many people. The flow of traffic increased dramatically during the 1950s and 60s, and the position was watched more and more anxiously. In 1967 the Bridge Trust brought down a consultant to advise them on the condition of the Bridge. It was found that rain-water was seeping through the two pavements, and was rusting the reinforcing rods; there was also a crack right across the last arch on the western end. Repairs were carried out at a cost of about £30,000.

In June of the same year the Feoffees discussed the future of the bridge with the Charity Commissioners, and wrote a letter to the Minister of Transport, Barbara Castle, asking her terms to take over the bridge as part of the Trunk Roads system, as the A39 connected with the bridge at each end.

In 1946 this suggestion had come from the Ministry, who wished to include the bridge in the Trunk Roads Act. At that time the Bridge Trust, backed by the Council, was reluctant to break with tradition; they also realised that all their property, comprising a large part of the town, would pass to a government depart-ment and might come under the control of a body with no local knowledge. In addition, they felt that once all their finan-cial assets had been passed over to the Ministry any urgent or costly repairs for the bridge would have to take their place in the queue with all other trunk roads under the Act. The Ministry's suggestion was successfully resisted, the Bridge Trust having given the assurance that it had the funds to keep the bridge in repair and that it could carry trunk road traffic safely and effectively.

In the late 1960s the increase in size and numbers of the vehicles using the bridge far out-stripped the vision of those Feoffees who acted in 1946. In the light of the previous widen-ing of 1924-25, they were accustomed to vehicles around five

Left: this unique photograph shows masonry actually falling into the Torridge. Only the narrow pinnacle on the right holds up the roadway.

Below: the two westernmost arches after the first collapse on 9th January 1968.

feet wide, which when passing each other on the sixteen feet wide carriageway of the bridge, had a width clearance of about three feet each side. As the width of vehicles gradually increased to over eight feet, two large vehicles trying to pass each other had to mount the pavements. These are carried by corbels, designed to take only the weight of pedestrians. The Feoffees sought the Ministry's permission to erect notices on the bridge, warning that it was dangerous for vehicles to mount the pavements, but were refused.

Another cause for concern was the vibration of heavy diesel-powered vehicles waiting at the traffic lights at the western end; fears had been frequently voiced for the safety of the arches immediately underneath.

No reply to the Feoffees letter of June 1967 had been received by 9th January 1968; in the late evening of that day two arches at the western end of the bridge began to collapse into the water. Few people knew anything about the accident until next morning they found themselves cut off from their work on either side of the Torridge, the bridge having been closed to traffic of any sort.

The bridge carried the trans-Atlantic cable, water and high-pressure gas mains. There was a real danger that if it collapsed completely these connections would be severed, with the possibility of a gas explosion. Engineers worked day and night; the gas main served the whole of the west of the town, including Northam, Westward Ho! and Appledore, and emergency arrangements were made for those people who might find themselves without gas for heating and cooking.

A ministry expert, and others concerned, met on the spot and discussed the immediate steps to be taken. These included building a foot-bridge from the quay to the undamaged portion of the bridge; from this would be slung pipes for the gas main. This bridge was in position within nine days of the disaster.

The next step was to effect a temporary repair for cars and buses, with heavy vehicles severely restricted. Until then, traffic wanting to cross the Torridge had to travel via Torrington, a round trip of about twenty miles.

On January 24th there was a tragedy; the foreman on the job, Tommy Mordey of Mansfield, was killed by a falling crane.

Renewed pressure was put on the Ministry of Transport to supply a new bridge over the river, but the Ministry pointed

The roadway was severed and the work of demolishing and removing the collapsed arches began.

49

Above: The second section of the temporary footbridge being slung into position.

Right:Temporary baulks of timber were placed on these girders for traffic to start crossing again on 29th March 1968.

out that this could not have priority over other trunk road improvements, and reminded the Bridge Trust that full responsibility for the maintenance of the Bridge lay with them.

It was clear that no-one could have got on more quickly with the job of temporary repair, and of the supply of a new footbridge, than did the Bridge Trust after the collapse.

A steel support was built under the west end of the bridge, and the two broken arches were demolished and removed.

Girders were laid for a new roadway from the undamaged portion of the bridge to the strengthened end of the quay; this temporary roadway was completed by the end of March 1968.

These repairs were so designed that the two arches could be rebuilt as before, but the roadway was more widely splayed at the western entrance to improve the flow of traffic.

On 21st March Barbara Castle announced that the Ministry would take over all repairs and future maintenance of the bridge backdated to 9th January, the day of the partial collapse. Compensation by the Bridge Trust would be on terms to be agreed later.

3

THE

CHURCH

St Mary's Church at the end of
the nineteenth century.

Bideford Parish Church

St Mary's Church, about 1837

n 1066 William the Conqueror gave to his wife, Matilda, the advowson and the Manor of Bideford, which had belonged to Britric. The advowson was the right to recommend a member of the clergy to high office in the parish. After Matilda's death in 1083 it was bestowed on Richard de Granville or Grandeville, for his services to the Crown. In the twelfth century it passed to Tewkesbury Abbey, and just over 100 years later it was acquired by another Richard de Granville, Lord of the Manor of Bideford. It remained to the Grenvilles until the family estates were broken up in 1744, when it was acquired by George Buck of Daddon, ancestor of the Stucleys. Having passed down this

54

family, the advowson was finally bought in 1932 by the Dioscesan Board of patronage and the Bideford Parochial Church Council.

There is evidence in the "Calendar of State Papers" in the British Museum that a Saxon church existed in Bideford in 1232. It may have been quite old at that date, because a new church was built around this smaller Saxon church circa 1259, and was dedicated by Bishop Bronescombe. The first recorded mention of St Mary as the church's patron saint is in the Archiepiscopal Register for 31st May 1504: "The Church of the Blessed Virgin Mary, Bideford."

Early Saxon Church

The reason for building the new church around the original Saxon one was so that services could go on, uninterrupted, during the reconstruction.

This new building was cruciform in design, and was built of local stone. It underwent a great many changes over the years, and finished up with three galleries, so that it looked "more like a lecture hall than a church". in 1728 it was repaired, with financial help from the Bridge Trust. The Corporation of Bideford gave an organ, and contributed £20 a year for the organist. By 1862 the church was found to be in a dangerous condition, and was pulled down. It was at this stage that traces of the earlier Saxon church were found by the architect.

Early English Church

During the rebuilding, many of the old stones were taken away and used in private houses (some having been returned to the church in the twentieth century) and all that was left of the mediaeval church was the tower, the Norman font, and possibly the stoup. The font had suffered great misfortune; during the Reformation it had been thrown out of the church, and in John Watkins' own words: "one . . . of these

The New Church, 1862-65

55

The Norman font once served as a pig trough.

Relations between Church and Corporation

impious reformers, to show his zeal more conspicuously, appropriated it (the font) to the purpose of a trough for his swine to feed out of; and if he had his deserts, he would have made one of their company."

Inside the church is a monument to one of the Grenville family, Sir Thomas Graynfyld; this escaped vandalism when the early church was pulled down.

The inscription reads: "Here lies Thomas Grauntvild, Knight, patron of this Church, who died the eighteenth day of March, in the year of our Lord 1513. On whose soul God have mercy, Amen".

There has long been happy co-operation between the Parish Church and the Mayor and Corporation, broken only by two unusual disputes.

In 1522, when Sir Roger Grenville was Lord of the Manor, the Rector of Bideford and the Bridge Wardens disagreed as to who should receive the offerings given to the two chapels on the bridge. Sir Roger appealed to the Bishop, who in 1523 awarded them to the Rector.

In 1742, the Rev John Whitfield became Rector, and he began incessant warfare with the Mayor and Corporation, which he kept up for forty years. On one occasion he broke open the Council's Record Room and took away all the documents that belonged to the Council and to the Bridge Trust. Unbelievably, he placed the body of a dead child in the room, and left it there for several months. An application was made to the Court of the King's Bench, as a result of which Rev Whitfield was ordered to pay prosecution costs (£60), and to return all the documents, to have the doors repaired, and to "remove the dead corpse, which he had wilfully and passionately placed there, to the infinite astonishment and scandal of the whole parish." Both parties agreed to keep peace with each other, but the Rector continued his aggressions. The Rev

Roger Granville, writing in 1883, went so far as to say "Mr. Whitfield was, unhappily for the welfare of the parish, spared to a very old age, not dying until the spring of 1783."

A t the time of the Conquest, Britric, as well as holding the advowson of Bideford, also held that of Northam, which passed in 1261 to the same Prior of Frampton in Dorset. The living passed through various patrons, and in 1788 it came into the gift of the Dean and Canons of Windsor with whom it remains.

Northam Parish Church

The Wesleyan Chapel in Bridge Street nearing completion about 1892.

I t is thought that there was a church in Northam as far back as the twelfth century, because the first pillar from the west end of the present building supports a Norman capital. This is the only trace of a Norman church that can be found. North of the church is a field called "Sentry", said to be a corruption of "Sanctuary", suggesting that a former church stood there.

Early Church

Among the ancient records of St Margaret's Church is a contract, signed on 1st June 1593. This was for building the new north aisle, which completely altered the shape of the church: until then the structure was cruciform. On one of the capitals of a pillar in the main aisle are these words: "This yele was made in Anno 1593", referring to the north aisle.

Restoration of the church in 1846-60

The Rev. Isaac Gosset was appointed Vicar in 1844, and he made a detailed survey of the Church before planning its restoration; he found it in a very dilapidated state. Among other troubles he reported that "the roofs (were) . . . covered with the smallest and cheapest slates, which blew off whenever there was a gale of wind . . . The chancel had a very old Early English roof. It was boarded over and white-washed with a wretched attempt at painting over the communion enclosure."

Unfortunately, Mr. Gosset took a dislike to the pulpit, not realising that it was Jacobean or even earlier. He complained that: "the old oak pulpit . . . harmonised badly with the Gothic tracery of the Church generally, so we were glad to get a stone one in its place." This beautiful "three decker pulpit" with its panels of marguerites, was torn out and sold. By the merest chance it was traced during World War Two to Wellington College by Mrs Payne Cook, wife of a former Vicar of Northam. The ancient oak had been used for a sideboard. It was sent to

Exeter to be restored, ready to be returned to St Margaret's; but after weeks of hard work, the pulpit was almost completed when it was destroyed by a bomb in an air raid on Exeter.

A priceless possession of St Margaret's Church is its Kyries. When the first English prayer-book was introduced in 1549, an order was made that all the old Latin forms (or Kyries) must be destroyed. The people of Devon and Cornwall were greatly opposed to the English version, and took up arms to resist it. The rebellion was put down, and many rebels were killed.

The Northam Kyries

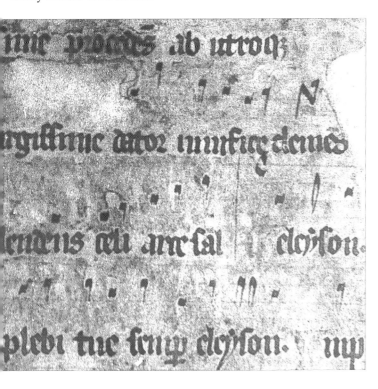

Part of the Northam Kyries.

Northam's copy of the Kyries was found in 1933, having been used as a wrapper around some churchwardens' accounts dated 1562. The Kyries are thought to date from the fourteenth century and to be the actual words and music as sung in Northam Church when Edward III was king.

Dissenters

Bideford gave shelter to a large number of Huguenots after the terrible massacre of St Bartholomew in France in 1572, and in the seventeenth century. Many of the refugees were weavers; they set up trade locally in cotton, silk and woollen goods. Elizabeth le Marchant de St Michel, daughter of a Bideford Huguenot, married Samuel Pepys the diarist in 1655.

Bideford was strongly Puritan in outlook, and welcomed the 1642 Act which abolished Church Government by bishops. In 1648, the Rev Arthur Gifford was dispossessed of his living of St Mary's Parish Church, and the Rev William Bartlett, lecturer, was put in his place. He preached Independency, and soon got a large following. After the Restoration, the Act of Uniformity of 1662 required every minister to declare publicly his assent to everything in the Book of Common Prayer. Among many others, William Bartlett was unable to make this declaration and was ejected in his turn, the Rev Arthur Gifford being reinstated.

Rev Bartlett, with his son John, began preaching in private houses in the district, for which they were both imprisoned. In 1694, after William of Orange had passed the Act of

Toleration in England, a Dissenting Chapel was built in Bideford, known as the "Little Meeting".

The "Little Meeting"; the first Dissenting Chapel to be built in Bideford.

In 1753, the Rev Samuel Lavington was ordained to the "Great Meeting," built in Bridgeland Street, where he ministered for fifty-four years; during his last twelve years he was helped by his son-in-law, the Rev Samuel Rooker.

Between the years 1854 and 1869 the "Great Meeting" was demolished and a new building completed, on the same site, called after Lavington.

BIDEFORD CHURCHMEN!!!

LOOK AT THIS:

"A very characteristic ebullition of High-church principles took place at Bideford on Saturday last. "The late Mr. Binney, of the Commercial Inn, who had been accustomed to attend with his family at the "Independent Meeting, was on that morning buried in the churchyard. The Curate of the parish "(the Rev. W. Braithwaite) and the Independent Minister (the Rev. J. T. Beighton) were therefore *both*, "though the fact was unknown to either, invited to lead the funeral procession—the friends of the deceased "in this act only obeying the law of usage, for from time immemorial the conforming and non-conforming "ministers of the town had thus walked as occasion required. In the present case however, when the Curate "discovered his *heretic brother* at his side, with the suavity of a Chesterfield, and the intolerance of a Laud, "he directed Mr. Beighton to a place among the friends, "for he could not recognise him," and therefore "should not walk with him." Unwilling to break into the solemnities of the scene by debate or resistance, "Mr. Beighton immediately bowed, and after reporting to the undertaker the reason, walked home. "As might have been expected, the incident occasioned no small excitement in the town, and "the conduct of the Curate was denounced in every quarter, and by none with more vehemence than the "members of his own congregation. In the name of the Dissenters in the town, Mr. Rooker applied to the "Rector for his opinion of the Curate's conduct, intimating that the insult was understood as being offered to "Mr. Beighton in his official capacity, and was therefore an insult offered to all the Dissenting Ministers of "the town, and through them to their respective congregations, comprising at least one-half the inhabitants "of the place. The Rector in reply in effect justified the Curate, but referred Mr. Rooker to him for a " "satisfactory explanation." The explanation was sought and received—Mr. Braithwaite, as a true son of the "church, could not and would not recognise Mr. Beighton, as a Minister. Had Henry of Exeter, or even "Onderdonk of New York, the convicted drunkard and debauchee, laid his hand on Mr. Beighton's head, "Mr. Braithwaite would have allowed him the privilege of a place at his side in a *funeral cortege !* Let "Mr. Braithwaite remember he is not living in the middle ages, and that such assumptions are but widening "the already broad and deep gap between the clergy and laity of his own church."

(*"Western Times,"* February 14*th* 1846.)

BIDEFORD CHURCHMEN! These are facts, and the dogma they indicate you cannot mistake. It assigns one half the people of this town to "the unco-venanted mercies of God," and treats their Pastors as "wolves in sheep's clothing." It hails as apostolically descended a Marsh of Peterborough, and a Cresswell of Creech St. Michael; but tells you that the SAMUEL LAVINGTON, whose memory you revere, the ROBERT HALL who numbered College Fellows and Tutors of Cambridge among his stated hearers, and the JOHN WILLIAMS who christianised tribes of his race, were not Ministers of Christ, but deluded and deluding men! It disdains to "recognise" the venerable JAY whose sermons have been reproduced in Episcopal Pulpits, and a CHALMERS at whose feet the noblest, the wisest and the holiest would gladly sit! The same dogma, in different times, reared the Inquisition Courts, and kindled the fires of Smithfield!

BIDEFORD CHURCHMEN! Will you *justify* the Act? Will you DEFEND it? Can you TOLERATE it? You claim, you HAVE the right of private judgment: speak: let your opinion be FELT: prove that you have "more understanding than your Teachers," more charity for your neighbours, and real desire for the brother-hood of this Town.

FEBRUARY, 16th 1846.

Printed at BISHOP'S General Printing Office, Mill-Street, BIDEFORD.

In 1662 the Rev Anthony Down was ejected from the Parish Church at Northam, and started preaching secretly at Appledore. For several years, services were held in a barn, which later was licensed for preaching; soon afterwards, a meeting house was built.

It seems, therefore, that both in Bideford and in Northam, the first bold Dissenters of English nationality were Congregationalists.

Northam and Appledore

Left: the Hill Garden Hotel in Mill Street was demolished in 1934 to provide a site for the Baptist Chapel.

Far left: the result of the Curate's refusal to walk with the dissenting Minister at a funeral in 1846!

The Rev Jerome Clapp, father of the author Jerome K Jerome, was Congregational Minister of Appledore in the early nineteenth century. He started a printing works in Odun Road, and as well as printing handbills, tickets, etc, he turned out books for his Sunday School. He called the works "The Congregational Tract Society".

The Congregational Tract Society

4

•••

SEA DOGS

Sir Richard Grenville

A panel made up of oak pew-ends from the ancient church of St Mary's showing the Grenville coat-of-arms and a member of the Grenville family.

Bideford's greatest hero was Sir Richard Grenville, born in June 1542, cousin to Sir Walter Raleigh, and descendant of the Richard de Granville who obtained the Charter for the town in 1272. Sir Richard always had a great love of adventure, and at the age of 22 he became a Crusader, returning in 1568 to help put down a rebellion in Ireland.

Five years later, he prepared an expedition to look for the Pacific end of the North West Passage, hoping at the same time to find the continent called Terra Australis, thought to lie in the South pacific. But the Government refused to let him go on this expedition, for fear of causing trouble with Spain, with whom England had an uneasy peace. So Sir Richard turned his attention to Bideford; in 1573 he obtained a Charter of Incorporation for the town from Queen Elizabeth the First. He organised defences in the West Country for the war with Spain that he knew would come eventually.

In 1585 he commanded a fleet of seven ships carrying West Country colonists to America; through his colonization of Carolina and

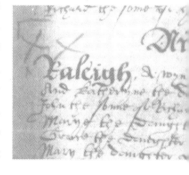

Virginia Sir Richard built up a flourishing trade in tobacco and other products between Bideford and New England, that was to last for almost 200 years.

Sir Richard's most unexpected import was a Red Indian servant – probably the first native American ever to come to England, whom he called after his cousin Raleigh. Perhaps the man pined for his homeland, or found the English winter too damp – for he only survived one year.

During Sir Richard's many voyages he never missed a chance of despoiling Spanish ships or colonies, bringing back booty to Queen Elizabeth. Early in 1588, he was ready with his fleet to return to Virginia, only awaiting "a faire winde". He received a letter from the Queen's Privy Council, which commanded him to "forbeare his intended voyage" and be ready to join the Navy at Plymouth. Sir Richard took five of his ships from Appledore and joined Sir Francis Drake in his battle with the Spanish Armada.

In 1591 Sir Richard Grenville sailed to the Azores in his

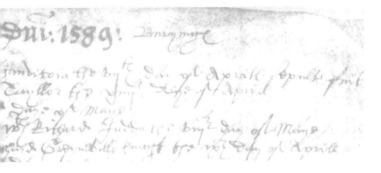

The entry in the Bideford Parish register of the Christening of Raleigh, the Wynganditoian Indian brought here by Sir Richard Grenville in 1588. According to the second entry in the register, the man died just one year later. He is now called "Rawly".

ship the Revenge, as second-in-command to Lord Thomas Howard, intending to waylay the Spanish treasure fleet on its way home. Somehow, Sir Richard got cut off from the rest of the English ships, and though he could have slipped away westwards, he decided to fight it out with his tiny force of 190 men, against fifteen Spanish ships and 5,000 men. Tennyson tells the rousing story in his poem "The Revenge". The fight lasted for fifteen hours, at the end of which, having inflicted tremendous losses on the enemy, Sir Richard was mortally wounded and surrendered. He was carried aboard the Spanish flag-ship, and died a few days later.

The replica of Sir Francis Drake's ship, Golden Hinde, which was built in Appledore in 1973.

A brass tablet to the right of the Lady Chapel in St Mary's Church records his epitaph: "SIR RICHARD GRENVILLE, Knight, Vice Admiral of England, aged 48. His last words, spoken in Spanish, were these:

'Here die I, Richard Grenville, with a joyful and a quiet mind, for that I have ended my life as a true soldier ought to do, fighting for his Country, Queen, Religion and Honour, my soul willingly departing from this body, leaving behind the lasting fame of having behaved as every valiant soldier is in duty bound to do.'"

After his death, a Spanish crew was put on the Revenge, which set sail for Spain; suddenly a storm blew up, and the ship was lost with all hands.

These great sailors were contemporaries of Sir Richard Grenville. They were born at Borough House, Northam; Stephen in 1526 and William ten years later. Living so near Appledore they were able to watch the ships in Appledore Pool, and probably got the sea in their blood at an early age. When Stephen was twenty-seven, he commanded the first English ship to reach Russia. While searching for the North East Passage to China, he found and named the North Cape, and on his next voyage he discovered the Kara Sea, to the extreme north-west of Russia. The following year he returned to the Kara Sea in the Searchthrift, looking for the Ob River, but weather conditions forced him to abandon the search. At the age of thirty-six, Stephen was made Chief Pilot of England; he died at Chatham at the age of 58. There is a memorial to him for his pioneering spirit at St Mary's Church, Chatham.

William and Stephen Borough

William Borough had sailed under his brother on these Arctic voyages, being only sixteen when he first signed on. Later, he commanded some of the ships belonging to the "Muscovy Company", engaged in trade with Northern Russia. He joined Martin Frobisher in his search for the North West Passage, and was often referred to by Frobisher as "my man Borrows".

He is best remembered for his skill as navigator, writer on nautical affairs, and cartographer. Some of his charts and maps can still be seen.

In 1583, William Borough became Comptroller of the Queen's Navy, and in 1587 was Vice-Admiral under Sir Francis Drake on his expedition to Cadiz. Borough died in 1599.

The original chart drawn by William Borough of Northam for use by Sir Martin Frobisher in his search for the North-East Passage to Cathay (China).

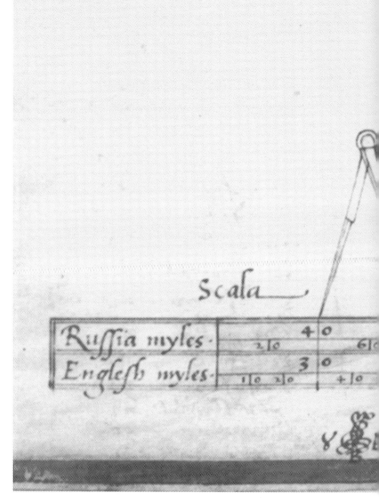

The press-gang

Since Edward III's Commission of Empressment in 1355, seamen lived in constant fear of the press-gang. In 1641, Parliament declared the system illegal, but Cromwell used it for his land and sea forces, as can be seen in an extract from the State Treasury Papers of April 1653.

A report to the Navy Commissioners reads:

"We have formed our orders for impressing mariners under the new Act with Captain Hatsell at Plymouth, and will put them into execution on the north side of Devonshire, about Bideford, Appledore, and Combe, where he assures us

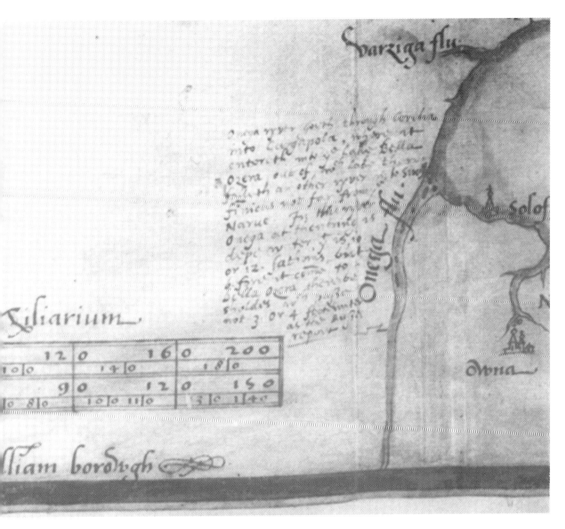

there are many seamen."

Two years later came the report: "February 27, 1655; Captain Henry Hatsell, Exeter, to Admiralty Commissioners. Has been to Barnstaple and Bideford, but could only get 24 seamen, they having fled out of the reach of the constables."

But local men were not always able to evade the hated press-gangs, and in 1656 Bideford claimed and was granted exemption from impressment for all men sailing on ships bound for Newfoundland, on account of the healthy trade that they were bringing to England.

5

●●●

BIDEFORD

QUAY

Bideford quay in 1884 looking north.
To the left of the lamp-post behind the
three girls is one of the Armada guns
which were used as bollards.

There must have been a quay of some sort for the use of ships trading with the Port of Bideford long before its first apparent mention in 1619. In this year, the second complaint against the Bridge Trustees was made to the Court of Chancery. It was alleged that John Sherman, Marriner, Warden and Receivor of the Bridge rents, in 1618 and 1619, "did detaine (the sum) in his hands, and refused to deliver and pay any part thereof towards the repayring, enlarging,

and building of the Key at Bydeford, adjoyning to the said Long Bridge, and for strengthening of the same, being a worke very chargeable, and for the genrall good of the Town and Parish of Bydeford aforesaid, and of the whole country."

This complaint implied that the original quay was built by the town, and in 1663 this was confirmed by an order for a new quay to be built, the money for it to be raised by gifts, supplemented by "fines made of the Bridge and Towne lands". A long list of regulations was issued, for the use of the quay by vessels, and for its care and upkeep by a "Water Bayliffe".

The quay before widening, and general view of the town, about 1885.

The Bridge Feoffees made a contribution to the widening in 1693, as an old account book shows:

"By cash to William Lennox for stones for building of 70 feet in length of the New Key and slip, and fitting the stones as by his articles of agreement . . . £ 60.0.0."

"To Nathaniel Gascoyne for building 200 feet of the Key and slip . . . £223.4.6.

This was in 1692, at the time of the development of Bridgeland Street.

Above: Bideford Quay in 1884.

Far right: the quay in 1905, after it was widened, showing almost complete lack of traffic and poorly surfaced road.

Right: the Pill Bridge was the only link between the quay and the river bank.

The quay was roughly 430 feet long, running from Cooper Street in the north to Conduit lane (which connects the quay to Allhalland Street) in the south. There was a slipway with steps half-way along, and another slip at the south end; stones have been let into the modern pavement marking these early limits.

In 1758 the Lord of the Manor extended the quay southwards to the bridge; it thus appears that it belonged to him at that period rather than to the town. John Watkins, writing in

1792, complained that the regulations for vessels using the quay, drawn up 1663, were being flouted by the Lord of the Manor, who "enjoys at present all these privileges, and farms them out to the best bidder; and the consequence is, that the owners of vessels are open to the most exorbitant impositions".

In 1828 an Act of Parliament was passed, making new regulations for the rates to be paid by users of the quay, which

To the Worshipful the MAYOR of BIDEFORD.

WE the undersigned Inhabitants of the Town of BIDEFORD, request that you will convene an early Meeting of the principal Inhabitants of the Town, for the purpose of taking into consideration the propriety of

Widening the North End
OF THE
PUBLIC QUAY,

As well for the purpose of benefitting the Town of BIDEFORD and Public in general, as for the paramount object of affording Employment to the Mechanics and Labourers who are now destitute of such employment.

BIDEFORD, December 22nd, 1840.

CHAS. CARTER	Robert Wren
Henry R. Glynn	J. Facey
Chas. A. Caddy	Fras. Ash
W. T. Hawke	Thos. L. Pridham
Thos. B. Chanter	John Hogg
Thos. Vellacott	T. H. Baller
Thos. Wickham	Philip Tardrew
R. C. Hamlyn	Thos. Balhatchet
James Haycroft	Geo. Richards
Thos. Chope	Rob. Taylor
W. C. Hatherly	W. H. Burnard
Chas. Smale	Thos. S. Heard
John Saunders	T. Griffith
S. C. Willcock	Wm. Wickham
S. C. Doidge	Jas. Rooker
Rob. Hamlyn	Wm. Cadd
Josias Wren	Geo. Braund
Henry Alford	

IN Pursuance of the above Requisition, I do appoint a PUBLIC MEETING to be held at the TOWN HALL, in *Bideford,*

On Monday, December 28th,
BY TWELVE O'CLOCK AT NOON.
THOS. LEY, Mayor.

DATED, December 24th, 1840.

HAYMAN, PRINTER, &c. BIDEFORD.

was then 1,200 feet long. At that time, the Lord of the Manor still claimed it as his property, but was having trouble in collecting his dues.

The Act did not help him to recover his money, however; on the contrary, he had to repair and improve the quay by widening it from Bridgeland Street to Conduit Lane, and this cost him £400.

Fourteen years later, further improvements were made, and a wooden bridge was placed across the Pill (the stream that joins the Torridge at the south end of the river bank). The last quay widening was in 1889-90. The following year a promenade was built down the length of the quay from the bridge to the river bank, and trees were planted all along it.

Above: the river bank before Victoria Park was opened in 1912.

Left: The narrowness of the quay gave continual concern to the traders of Bideford.

Armada guns

When the quay was widened, some of the mooring-posts that had to be removed were found to be guns. They had been placed there at the end of the nineteenth century. It was suggested that they might be Spanish guns, captured from the Armada.

The authorities decided to check on their origin, and in 1896 the Royal Artillery Institution

The Armada guns in 1909 next to the School of Art on the site of the present Post Office.

made a thorough examination of them, publishing a full report.

The conclusion reached was: "That it would be impossible for anyone who has studied the question to say definitely that the guns were not captured from the Spaniards in the sixteenth century.

"It is only reasonable to suppose that a port of the distinction of Bideford would become possessed of some of the guns captured from the Armada.

The paddle-steamer, the Privateer, ran pleasure trips from Bideford and other Bristol Channel ports at the end of the nineteenth century.

"These guns are not English, are of the sixteenth century, and four out of five correspond to authenticated (Armada) guns at Inverary. It is therefore more than probable that in these guns Bideford possesses ordnance captured from the Spanish Armada; but there is not sufficient proof to state this as an absolute fact".

After this delightfully indefinite conclusion, the guns were placed outside the Art School on the quay, and later removed to Victoria Park, where they can be seen today.

6

●●●

THE SEVENTEENTH CENTURY

Chudleigh Fort commands a good view of
River Torridge.

During the Civil War, Bideford, like many other Devonshire towns, was a stronghold of Puritanism, while most of Cornwall had Royalist sympathies. When the war began in 1642, the Parliamentarians of Bideford built three forts. One, West-the-Water, was possibly above what is now Torridge Hill; another, East-theWater and still standing, is called after Colonel James Chudleigh who was in command of the Parliamentary forces in Bideford at the time; the third was built on Staddon Hill, at Appledore, in a fine position overlooking the Taw / Torridge estuary.

In much of Bideford's history, events link her with

Chudleigh Fort about 1860 showing Robert Johnson's shipyard (later to become Restarick's) beyond the bridge, and also the entrance to the old paint mine

Barnstaple, and this is especially true of the Civil War. During the years 1642-45, Bideford and Barnstaple men marched side by side, sometimes armed only with scythes and pitch-forks.

Sir Bevil Grenville, grandson of the great Sir Richard, and a keen Royalist, had a town house at Bideford. In April, 1643, one of the authorised news sheets of the Parliamentarian party gave the account of a plot on Sir Bevil's part to sieze

Bideford for the King. Some of his soldiers were to enter Bideford dressed as "countrimen", and were to mix with Royalist sympathisers in the town, cutting the throats of the Watch, and then letting in Sir Bevil's regiment.

The account goes on: "but it pleased God in his mercifull providence to discover the treachery thus; one of the Conspirators being a Townsman hapned to be drunk the afternoon before that dismal night, and in his drunkenesse openly babbled what feates he and the rest of his complices meant to performe the night following."

Thus the plot was discovered and foiled; the historians consider it to be just one of the numerous scares of the period.

Sir Bevil lost his life fighting with great courage at Lansdowne, near Bath, in July 1643.

Battles raged back and forth across the West Country, and Torrington was twice occupied by Royalist troops. On the second occasion, in July 1643, Colonel Digby was in command. The Parlia-

This beautiful plaster mantelpiece originally stood in Sir Bevil Grenville's town house on the quay (now a shop) and shows the Grenville Arms and Sir Bevil himself. It was covered by panelling for many years after the house became the Three Tuns Inn.

mentarians of Bideford and Barnstaple launched an attack on Digby's men, and suffered heavy losses. They retreated to Bideford, where the Royalists laid siege to them. Barnstaple sent money to Bideford "for corne and powder to incourage them to hold out against ye siedge of Coll. Digby", but Bideford surrendered on promise of a pardon. Two months later Barnstaple, too, was taken by the Royalists. In 1644, Barnstaple rose against its small Royalist garrison, and having gained possession of the town, attacked the King's men who were holding the fort at Appledore. This foray must have been by boat, as it is only seven miles down river from Barnstaple.

The attack proved unsuccessful, and a party of the King's horse and foot was sent from Exeter to subdue Barnstaple.

In 1646, a fresh wave of Parliamentarians under Sir Thomas Fairfax and Oliver Cromwell reached North Devon; Torrington fell, and 200 Royalist prisoners were shut up in the church. Unhappily, it was also their arsenal, though Fairfax didn't realise this. The powder exploded, and blew up the church and some of the property around it, killing all the prisoners. Barnstaple was besieged for five weeks, and surrendered in April. Bideford must have surrendered at about the same time, although the date is not known.

The Plague

Before Bideford had time to recover from the effects of civil war, she was hit by a worse enemy – pestilence. In June 1646, a ship importing wool from Spain was discharging her cargo on the quay; three children, the sons of a Bideford surgeon called Ravening, are said to have been playing on the sacks. All three died of plague a few days later, doubtless from infected wool. As Watkins puts it, the disease "dissused itself to so shocking a degree, that in a few weeks the houses were filled with horror and the streets covered with grass".

The Parish Register dates the plague from June 8th to January 18th, but no mention is made of the deaths of the Ravening boys, nor of a "George Forgitt", whose names were inscribed on their gravestones with the chilling words: "IN THE DESEAS DIED HEE". The omission of these names from the register seems to imply that many more victims died than

Above: Sir Thomas Fairfax.

Right: John Strange. The background shows incidents in which he narrowly escaped death; he fell off a cliff when bird-nesting as a boy; was hit on the temple by an arrow, which left a permanent scar; and was thrown over the low bridge parapet by a robber. He was believed to have been protected by Providence to save Bideford from the plague of 1646.

could be registered.

The Mayor (who was not named) fled in terror. John Strange, a wealthy merchant and previous Mayor, who lived at Ford House, took over responsibility. He put guards at the entrances to the town to prevent the spread of infection; he saw that the sick were cared for; he arranged for the burial of the dead, and comforted the bereaved. At the height of the infection he died of the plague himself, and was buried on July 30th, 1646.

A sea captain, befriended by Strange, returned to Bideford to reward him, and learned of his death. He erected a monument to him, which still stands in St Mary's Church.

In his will, Strange gave five houses in Meddon Street, with gardens, for the use of "Poor Old People".

Local Charities

In this era of great wealth on the one hand, and abject poverty on the other, it was usual for rich merchants to settle money on the needy. Perhaps the best known in Bideford is John Andrew's Dole. By his will of 1605, the rent of a field was to be used for the "relief of the poor".

This charity still exists. The original field is in the ownership of trustees who distribute the rent, on New Year's Day, to "the poor and needy of Bideford" in accordance with the terms of John Andrew's will.

THE
Tryal, Condemnation, and
EXECUTION
OF THREE
WITCHES,
VIZ.
TEMPERACE FLOYD,
MARY FLOYD,
AND
SUSANNA EDWARDS.

Who were Arraigned at *Exeter* on the 18th, of *August*, 1682. And being prov'd Guilty of Witch-Craft, were Condemn'd to be Hang'd, which was accordingly Executed in the view of many Spectators, whose strange and much to be lamented Impudence, is never to be forgotten.

Also, how they Confessed what Mischiefs they had done, by the assistance of the Devil, who lay with the above-named *Temperance Floyd* Nine Nights together. *Also,* how they Squeezed one *Hannah Thomas* to death in their Arms; How they also caused several Ships to be cast away, causing a Boy to fall from the top of a Main-Mast into the Sea.

With many Wonderful Things, worth your Reading.

Printed for *J. Deacon,* at the sign of the *Rainbow,* a little beyond St. *Andrews* Church, in *Holborn.* 1682.

The best known charity in Northam is Melhuish's gift, which was mainly money invested to encourage education.

In 1682, three Bideford women were convicted of witchcraft at Exeter Assizes, and executed. They were Temperance Lloyd, Mary Trembles and Susannah Edwards. The account of their trial shows that they were helpless in the face of spite, ignorance and credulity.

Watkins commented, a century later: "The belief of witchcraft remained very general in the town and neighbourhood, and there was always some poor devil, either on account of an unlucky visage, sour temper, or wretched poverty, set up as the object of terror and universal hatred, till about twenty years since." This shows how comparatively short a time has passed since innocent people could suffer such a savage fate in England.

The Bideford Witches

Left: the frontispiece of pamphlet telling the story of the three Bideford witches.

Below: this cottage in Old Town is thought to have been the home of the three Bideford witches. It was burned down in 1894.

7

●●●

INDUSTRY

The dedication of the mission ship
Edward Birkbeck in 1880. This was the
last ship to be built at Restarick's
ship-yard.

Ship building

t is thought that ships were built in Bideford and Appledore as far back as the fourteenth century. John Leland, the first English antiquary, wrote in 1533 that Bideford had "a praty quik streate of Smithes and other occupiers for ship crafte". From Weare Giffard down to West Appledore the sound of hammers and smell of tar told of a thriving industry and a crowded port.

Many types of vessels were built, including merchant ships for the trade with Maryland and Virginia in the sixteenth century; armed merchant ships for the Newfoundland trade 100 years later; ships for transporting convicts to Botany Bay around 1700; warships for the Royal Navy during the Napoleonic Wars and also World War II; and many hundreds of smaller vessels of all types.

Some of the well-known names were HM Restarick, who took over Johnson's ship-yard near the east end of the bridge in 1877; Thomas Waters, also East-the-Water, near Cross Park (afterwards the Railway Goods Station); William Brooks, next door; George Crocker's ship-yard on the bank of the Pill at the bottom of Willett Street; and Chapman and Ellis, at Cleave

Far left: these vessels were known as bomb ketches, and were built in Bideford at Chapman's Shipyard, Cleave Houses, from 1800 to 1814.

Left: Cleave Houses with shipyard and lime-kiln at the beginning of the twentieth century.

Below: Restarick's Shipyard, East-the-Water, in the 1870s, now Brunswick Wharf.

Above: a forest of masts at Appledore Quay, about 1875, The ship in the centre has double clad sides to protect it when berthing against harbour walls.

Right: the "Donkey House" at Cox's Shipyard, which was later turned into a concrete works and finally demolished to make way for Torridge District Council's head offices.

Far right: the Torridge in 1946, choked with war-surplus ships. The tower, Chanter's Folly, was built in the early nineteenth century by Thomas Chanter, so he could watch his ships come in over the bar, and could summon casual labour to be ready to unload them. It was demolished in 1952.

Houses, River Bank, later taken over by Evans and Cox. This yard closed down in 1877, and in 1919 was converted for building steel vessels by the Hansen Ship-building Company. The slump in shipping caused the closure of the yard in 1924.

At Appledore, William Yeo from Prince Edward Island built Richmond Dry Dock in 1855; many ships came from the Island to Appledore to be fitted, and Yeo became a wealthy and influential man. Robert Cock had a ship-yard near what is now the Seagate Hotel, and other well-known ship-builders were William Clibbet, Thomas Geen, H Hinks, Peter Cook and PK Harris.

In 1973 a replica of Sir Francis Drake's flagship, the Golden Hinde, was made at Hinks's yard, and is now in dry dock in Southwark, London, next to the replica Globe Theatre.

There were seven limekilns along the River Torridge from Bideford to Appledore, and nine above the bridge, as well as some along the sea-coast. Culm (a form of anthracite) was used for the fires. The lime produced was used by farmers as an early type of fertiliser, but the coming of artificial manures at the end of the nineteenth century killed the industry.

Limekilns

Rolle Canal

In 1823, Lord Rolle cut a canal to carry goods from the River Torridge to Torrington. This was followed two years later by the building of the Rolle Canal Ship-yard at Sea Lock, on the west side of the river, opposite Weare Giffard. Only the hulls of the vessels were built there; they were brought down through the widest arch of the bridge and the masts, etc, were

Main picture: the aqueduct near Torrington, from a print of 1823 celebrating the opening of the Rolle Canal.

Right and below: to avoid a series of locks, the barges were manoeuvred up and down a ramp of rollers by a chain hoist.

fitted afterwards. These ships were built for the general coastal trade in coal from Wales, limestone, culm, and so on, then to be sent up the new canal. Lord Rolle spent a great deal of money on the developments connected with the canal, including an aqueduct over the river at Beam; a large mill, limekilns, an iron foundry, and a stone bridge joining Torrington with Little Torrington.

At about the same time another ship-building yard was

built near the Halfpenny Bridge at Weare Giffard.

With the extension of the railway from Bideford to Torrington in 1870, transport passed from the canal, and its brief day was over.

Rope-making

Rope-works could always be found near yards that built wooden sailing ships.

There was a rope-walk at the end of Bideford river bank, near Cox's Yard, and another at the back of New Street, in Appledore. The present Rope Walk in Bideford marks the site of a third; here, ropes were stretched around posts all the way down the Strand, from the shed (see photo on opposite page) to the gate of Northdown House.

The coming of the age of steam brought decline to both these industries, and in 1886 the Strand rope-works were sold to make way for a collar factory.

Local people rebelled against the removal of the ancient posts,

but the development went ahead, although some of the posts remained there for many years.

Main picture: in 1886, when the rope factory closed down, the local inhabitants protested at the removal of the old posts around which ropes were stretched.

Far left: the posts remained in the Strand for some years after they ceased to be used.

Below: Rope Walk in the 1880s, with the shed, on the left of the picture, where the ropes were made until 1886.

Potteries

Below: Green's china shop in High Street about 1887, on the site of the present Lloyds bank.

Right: examples of Bideford pottery. The mug on top is an unusually delicate white with floral design; the others are typical of Bideford yellow sgrafitto ware.

Bideford had potteries in medieval times, making tiles for church floors. J Phillips of Newton Abbot, writing in 1881, says that Bideford tiles were used in Down St Mary Church, Devon. The tiles were usually in a fleur-de-lis pattern, in relief. Phillips claimed that: "Bideford ovens have been known all through the West of England and South Wales from time immemorial."

At one time there were five potteries in Potter's Lane (now North Road), backing on to what used to be a beach, and is now the Strand. Barges brought clay from Fremington and discharged it where the Bideford Bowling Club is now.

A pottery in Torrington Lane was demolished in 1920, and

there was another at Cleave Houses, near Chircombe; the
North Devon Pottery at Annery was found to have the date
"1609" inscribed on its chimney. These old kilns were open at
the top, with the hole covered with old crocks.

Bideford potters were well known for their sgraffito ware;
in this, the pattern is scratched through a slip of pipe clay over
red earthenware. A lead glaze is used, resulting in a combina-
tion of brilliant yellow and reddish brown. Harvest jugs,
mugs, money boxes, dishes and bowls were turned out in pro-
fusion. During the seventeenth century, large quantities of
Bideford and Barnstaple pottery were exported to North
America.

Right: The old pottery in Torrington
Lane, which closed in 1917.

Below: The last Bideford potter at work
in Torrington Lane in 1915.

Port of Bideford

Bideford's overseas trade had increased so greatly by the early seventeenth century that she applied for a Custom House. Despite the protests of Barnstaple who already dealt with bonded goods, the petition was granted, and a Custom House was established at the bottom of Bridgeland Street. As Barnstaple had feared, Bideford's trade increased even more, and at the beginning of the eighteenth century the town imported more tobacco than any other port in the country. The discarded tobacco hogsheads were used as refuse bins – Bideford was the first town to organise street refuse collections in this way.

Wool was imported from Ireland, salted cod from Newfoundland, wine from the Mediterranean, whilst cotton and woollen goods, linen, spirits, cordage and many other commodities were exported to the colonies.

In 1711, France started to show an interest in the Newfoundland trade, and this competition, coinciding with the plundering of Bideford's laden merchant ships by French privateers lurking off Lundy, brought disaster to the local merchants.

The war with France, followed in 1775 by the American War of Independence, cut off all Bideford's trade with Newfoundland and the colonies.

In 1886 Bideford temporarily lost the title of "Port", and was included with Barnstaple under the Customs Consolidation Act, but after frequent protests by local people, the privilege was restored in 1928.

Top far left: the old Custom House at Appledore in 1904, near what is now the Richmond Dock.

Bottom far left: the journey from Bideford to Exeter by coach in 1833 took seven and a half hours, barring mishaps on the road.

Left: a horse-bus at the bottom of High Street at the turn of the nineteenth and twentieth centuries.

Below: these livery stables stood at the end of the New Road to Torrington, on the site where the library now stands.

8

THE VICTORIANS
AND AFTER

Westward Ho! Ladies' Golf Club in 1873.

The impact of the Victorian age on Bideford and district changed its character for ever. The pioneering spirit that drove John Hanning Speke, of Orleigh Court, Bideford, to his difficult search for the source of the Nile; the bombast of Charles Chappell who put up the stone at Bloody Corner and had his own name incised on it; the ostentation of Thomas Chanter who built his "Folly" at Appledore, from which he could watch his ships sail in over the bar; the business enterprise

The Rev Charles Kingsley, 1819-1875.

that produced the railways: all these qualities were combined in the rapid development of the area.

In 1855, Charles Kingsley's book *Westward Ho!* was published, and became immensely popular. People looked with fresh vision at the neighbourhood he had portrayed as a boyhood haunt of Amyas Leigh, (until then known simply as 'Northam Burrows') and saw its potentiality as a fashionable watering-place.

In November 1863 a Mr Pynsent gave a "Penny Reading" (so much loved by the Victorians) called "Ye Past, Ye Present, and Ye Future of Ye Burrows of Northam". He eulogised the health and good looks of the inhabitants of Northam, and said, "Throughout the whole summer, and more especially on

Part of the property map of Westward Ho!, when the new developments came up for sale in 1907.

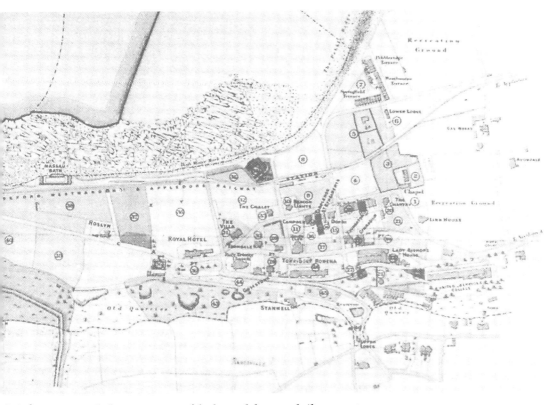

bright autumnal days, troops of lads and lasses daily resort to these Burrows." He went on to urge his audience to take up shares with the company that was going to develop the district.

An impressive list of wealthy local men formed the Board of Directors of this company, and in 1863 the foundation stone of the first villa was laid by the Earl of Portsmouth; at this ceremony the name "Westward Ho!" after Kingsley's book, was bestowed on the village. By 1872 it boasted a new church (Holy Trinity), a row of shops, and some terrace houses.

Royal North Devon Golf Club

The prospectus of the development company had described the Burrows as a wide expanse of smooth turf, 1,000 acres in all, adapted for cricketing, "and the Scotch game of golf". Here, no time had been wasted in laying out a golf course, and by 1863 the Royal North Devon Golf Club had been formed. The Rev Isaac Gosset was one of the founder members. This course soon became known as one of the best in the country.

Westward Ho! Pier

In 1864 the company planned a promenade pier, to be built out from Rock's Nose to the south west of the beach, "so that yachts may lie there in safety". The project was begun in 1870. Two years later the company reported, "All previous attempts to build a promenade pier failed, owing to the fury of the winter storms,

which washed the framework away." The engineer doing the work gave it up as hopeless, but a John Abbott of Bideford undertook to complete a shortened form of the pier. In 1874 the company congratulated the directors on their report, which promised that the new pier would be open in time for the summer season.

In 1880 came the report, "The late severe weather has been very disastrous to the pier. Two of the iron supporting legs gave way some time ago, and last week two more were broken off. The planking of the upper part is so rotten that it can hardly hold together much longer. Three months later came the brief final report, "It has been decided to remove the pier, which has become dangerous as well as unsightly." Some of the iron foundation posts can still be seen at low tide.

Left: Westward Ho! beach in the 1870s.

Below: the heyday of Westward Ho! pier in 1875. It was washed away five years later.

Bottom: the pier under construction in 1872.

United Services College

This school was opened at Westward Ho! in 1874 for the sons of officers, and occupied all the houses now comprising Kipling Terrace. They had been built as separate dwellings, and must have been very inconvenient for a school.

Rudyard Kipling was a pupil here from 1878, when he was twelve, until 1882. He was made editor of the *United Services College Chronicle* during his last two years. One of his books, *Stalky and Co*, is all about his schooldays at Westward Ho! By 1899 various factors combined to cause the governors to consider moving the school, and in 1904 it was transferred from Westward Ho! and was eventually re-established at Windsor.

Top: the United Services College as it was when Kipling went to school there.

Right: Kingsley College was founded for "sons of Noblemen and Gentlemen on Sound Church of England Principles". It only lasted a few years.

Far right: the Great Nassau Swimming Baths were originally built for the pupils of the United Services College. When the college moved in 1904 the Baths were opened to the public, and return ticket holders on the railway were admitted for 4d instead of 6d.

Coastal erosion and the pebble ridge

The development company was not at first aware of the increasing danger of coastal erosion at Westward Ho! – they found out the hard way.

In 1878 they reported that a new ridge of pebbles had been formed within the past two years; the weakest part of the pebble ridge being at the new Golf Club House, "which is built at the lower level, almost close to the sea". The company had a wooden breakwater, in the form of piles, driven into the ground in front of the Club House.

A year later the pebble ridge had been driven back about seventy feet, right

The pebble ridge was pushed back four hundred yards between 1872 and 1906 when these two photographs were taken. The Club House (centre of top picture) was pulled down in 1879 and rebuilt further from the sea.

under the windows of the Club House, and on one occasion the sea hurled these pebbles against the building with such force that the people who were inside rushed out in a panic. It was feared that "unless previously removed, the Club House will be swept away by the next high tides". Later in 1879 the Club House, having been surrounded several times by "spent waves", was actually undermined by the sea.

The need for a short sea wall was stressed, between "the Ladies Bath House and the Lower Lodge", but before it could be built the sea had reached Lower Lodge and it was removed and rebuilt further from the sea front.

In 1880, fresh storms caused 100 tons of embankment between the Baths and Pebble Ridge Terrace to be swept away.

In the early years of the twentieth century there was a spate of letters in the local press about the movement of pebbles, and the possible danger of erosion of the Burrows. The principal writers were Edwin Vidal and Inkerman Rogers. The latter believed that the pebbles were washed along from the cliffs towards the sandhills, and he started a series of experiments to prove his theory, by marking pebbles and then noting how far they had moved.

Top: foundations being dug for the Westward Ho! sea wall in 1928.

Above: a bridge helped holidaymakers reach the sands in the early 1920s.

In 1928, the sea wall was built at Westward Ho! since when, although severely battered by the sea from time to time, no more houses and land have been washed away.

Potwallopers and the Burrows

Northam parishioners, or Potwallopers as they are still called, have always had the right of grazing on the Burrows, which is common land. It used to be a custom for the Potwallopers to meet on Whit Monday, and spend the day throwing back the pebbles that the winter storms had tossed on to the Burrows. Charles Chappell, probably the keenest Potwalloper of all time, continually exhorted the local people to resume this annual clearance of the pebbles. He deeply resented anyone encroaching on the ancient rights of the Burrows by taking vehicular traffic on to the turf. When the golf course was laid out, small bridges were built over the streams that drained the land, and the golfers used to cross these in their carriages. On one occasion Chappell went to Appledore and talked to a group of sailors whose boats were laid up for the winter, so working on

Tenders.

THE NORTHAM BURROWS COMMITTEE

INVITE TENDERS for the REPAIR of the BREACH in the PEBBLE RIDGE at Sandy Meir, particulars of which may be obtained of Mr. F. WILKEY, Venton, Westward Ho! to whom tenders should be sent not later than 12 noon, Friday, the 13th day of March, 1925.

(Signed) F. WILKEY, Secretary.
Northam Burrows Committee.
Dated 7th March, 1925.

Right: an extract from Inkerman Rogers' notebook showing how he charted the movement of pebbles along the ridge away from Westward Ho!

Above: In the 1920s the Northam potwallopers repaired the pebble ridge theselves.

October 5. 1928. Groundswell. Wind off shore.
23 pebbles marked with tar and set on the pebble ridge opposite the sternpost of the wreck; 2 large pebbles 50 to 60 ll
October 14th All pebbles moved northeastward. Coarse gravel here.
October 15th Northwest wind.

1 pebble	5 lbs moved	50 ft	northeast direction into estuary
1 "	7 lbs "	47 ft	" " "
1 "	"	17 ft	" " "
1 "	"	15 ft	" " "
1 "	"	12 ft	" " "
2 pebbles	"	11 ft	" "
1 "	"	8 ft	" " "

1 pebble 60 lbs, & 3 smaller ones moved 10 ft " " " "
Four pebbles moved up the ridge two thirds of the way.
October 29. 20. N West to W winds. Rough sea. Spring tides. High tide on 30th inst. Small shingle drawn down and spread evenly over the face of the Ridge.

their feelings that they armed themselves with crowbars and pickaxes and followed him to the Burrows. There they destroyed the bridges, shouting that they were preserving "our property".

Chappell is said to have served a prison sentence for his part in the affair, and to have found himself a hero when he came out.

The first completed section of the sea wall. The groynes were soon worn down by the grinding of the pebbles

The Bideford, Westward Ho! and Appledore Railway

With the development of Westward Ho! came the need for easy transport from Bideford. A railway was suggested, but a great many years passed before it was finally agreed to build the standard gauge Bideford, Westward Ho! and Appledore Railway. The first part of the line was opened in 1901, and ran from Bideford Quay to Westward Ho!

The track started by following the course of the Pill, which had to be culverted and enclosed (the original cause of the flooding of Kenwith Valley in rainy weather). It ran along what is now Kingsley Road as far as Chanters Lane; then over the Causeway at the bottom of First Raleigh, along the Kenwith Valley straight out to Cornborough Cliffs, where it curved around into Westward Ho! station. The last part of the journey from Cornborough to Westward Ho! gave the most spectacular views of the sea and coast, but in stormy weather the engine had a job to pull the train around the point into the teeth of a gale.

During 1902, the railway company repeatedly pressed the Bideford Council to allow a loop-line to be built on the quay. This loop was required to run the engine around the train; without it the company needed to keep two engines in steam, even when running a reduced service. The council refused permission, but the company went ahead all the same, and

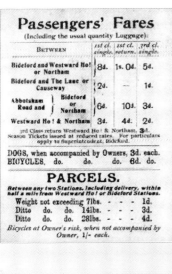

Passengers' Fares
(Including the usual quantity Luggage):

BETWEEN	1st cl. single.	1st cl. return.	3rd cl. single.
Bideford and Westward Ho! or Northam	8d.	1s. 0d.	5d.
Bideford and The Lane or Causeway	2d.	—	1d.
Abbotsham Road and } Bideford or Northam	6d.	10d.	3d.
Westward Ho! & Northam	3d.	4d.	2d.

3rd Class return Westward Ho! & Northam, 3d.
Season Tickets issued at reduced rates. For particulars apply to Superintendent, Bideford.

DOGS, when accompanied by Owners, 3d. each.
BICYCLES, do. do. do. 6d. do.

PARCELS.
Between any two Stations, including delivery, within half a mile from Westward Ho! or Bideford Stations.

Weight not exceeding 7lbs.	-	-	-	1d.
Ditto do. do. 14lbs.	-	-	-	3d.
Ditto do. do. 28lbs.	-	-	-	4d.

Bicycles at Owner's risk, when not accompanied by Owner, 1/- each.

BIDEFORD, WESTWARD HO!
AND
APPLEDORE RAILWAY COMPANY.

TIME TABLE
FROM
MAY 1st, 1902
(UNTIL FURTHER NOTICE).

Head Office—
DONINGTON HOUSE,   Superintendent's Office—
NORFOLK STREET,   THE QUAY,
STRAND,   BIDEFORD.
LONDON, W.C.

S. R. BOOTH,   HENRY SOWDEN,
Secretary.   Superintendent.

Coles and Owen, Printers, Bideford.

Far left: laying the railway line tramway fashion on Bideford Quay in 1901.

Left: it was more expensive to travel on the railway than go by horse-drawn brake.

Below: the Causeway level crossing.

one September Sunday morning, Bideford awoke to find navvies tearing up the quay to lay the loop. Next day, the Town Crier was sent out to call a protest meeting, which was attended by several hundred people. The meeting was told that the railway company "had not the interest of the town at heart, but their one idea and aim is to make money". This attitude of the townspeople is probably one of the reasons why the company never in fact did make money.

As a result of the meeting, the council obtained an injunction against the company, which was forced to remove the rails, but eight months later they were relaid, after the company had got the support of the Board of Trade.

In 1908, the line was extended to Appledore, a total distance of about seven and a half miles, but despite this increase to the service, the railway never paid its way, partly because

Below: laying the points of the loop line on Bideford Quay in the summer of 1903.

Top right: Westward Ho! station after the line had been extended to Appledore in 1908.

Bottom right: one of the sumptuously appointed coaches being assembled on the quay.

of the increasing cost of coal, and partly because it depended so heavily on the holiday season. When it was commandeered for use in France in World War I, the directors of the company must have been most relieved.

Traces of the old railway are

to find. The engine sheds in Kingsley Road are still used by local industry; the embankment at Kenwith and along the cliffs, although overgrown in places, is still well defined; and at West Appledore the main road passes through what used to be the station buildings which marked the end of the line.

Top left: the first train to reach Westward Ho! on 24th April 1901, was played in by a German band.

Top right: a special track was laid across the bridge when the last engine left for France in July 1917. The line was never reopened after the war.

Left: a motor bus service in Northam Square in 1918. These buses provided a quicker service than the railway ever did.

9

●●●

OLD BIDEFORD, NORTHAM AND APPLEDORE

Northam Square circa 1870

Buildings

The oldest house in Bideford is Old Ford House, formerly Ford Farm; it is believed to have been built in the sixteenth century, and possibly parts of it even earlier. It was added to in 1756. At one time the Grenvilles of Stowe (Cornwall) owned it.

The Royal Hotel, East-the-Water, was built in 1688 by John Davie, a wealthy merchant; it was known as the Colonial Buildings. The outside has been altered, but inside there is a fine late seventeenth century staircase, and two rooms on the first floor have good plaster ceilings.

In Northam, the outbuildings only of old Borough House remain. The rest was pulled down at the end of the nineteenth

A recruiting meeting with an
early armoured car in Northam Square
in 1914.

century, and the present house built on the site. Borough
House was the home of the sailor Boroughs; it was used in
Kingsley's *Westward Ho!* as the home of Amyas Leigh. Leighs
did actually inherit it in the sixteenth century.

The oldest house in Appledore is Docton House; this
stands in a courtyard at the bottom of Myrtle Street. It is said
to have been built by Cistercian monks in the fourteenth century, and was occupied by them until the Dissolution of the
Monasteries. Built of stone, with architraves and mullions of
red Cornish granite, until recently it still had fine plaster
friezes in Tudor Rose and fleur-de-lis design.

At the end of the sixteenth century the Doctons of Hartland

lived in the house, and presumably organised the passage of goods coming by sea to Hartland.

Here is part of an ancient record showing the devious route a ton of lead took from Bristol to Hartland Church:

"Pd. for a tunne of lead in Bristol   xiJI.

Pd. for custome for the same   ijs.

Pd. for fraight to Northam   vs.

Pd. for landing and carrying it into Mr. Docton's seller   xijd."

The lead was then loaded from Docton cellar to another boat at "Northam", and from thence to Clovelly Quay, from which it was shipped by still another boat to Hartland Quay, then carried up to the church.

Right: Fore Street, Northam, circa 1860.

Below right: Cross Street, Northam, about the same time.

Far right: High Street, Bideford, in the early years of the twentieth century.

128

Knapp House, between Northam and Appledore, was once the home of the notorious Thomas Benson, Member of Parliament for Barnstaple in 1749. He obtained a government contract to tranship convicts to the American colonies, and saved himself trouble and expense by landing them on Lundy, just twenty miles from Appledore. On the island, he used them as slaves, making them build great walls to improve the property. When his fraud was discovered, Benson successfully pleaded that he had fulfilled the terms of his contract by taking the convicts out of the country, for Lundy was just as much out of the world as the colonies.

His next attempt at fraud was to insure his ship, the

Nightingale, and then to land the cargo on Lundy; after this the ship was set on fire and abandoned. The captain was executed for this crime, and Benson fled to Portugal, guilt-ridden on account of the sufferings that had come on his crew through his greed. He never returned to Devon, but died in Portugal.

Bideford was well-supplied with prisons. In the late

eighteenth century French prisoners-of-war were "confined in a very close place" where the old gas works used to stand at Nutaberry, East-the-Water. For civil offenders there was a gaol in Meddon Street, which in 1831 was said to contain six cells "with glazed windows", presumably a refinement. In 1840, this prison was removed to part of the Colonial Buildings (now the Royal Hotel).

The grim sounding "prisoners' pit" surrounded by iron railings was on the site of the present Town Hall. In 1880 a report on Bideford's cells said: "The lock-ups are dark, deficient in ventilation, and wholly unfit places of detention for prisoners."

Streets and derivation of names

When Grenville Street was excavated for widening, a vein of culm was exposed, extending from the Rectory Gardens at the top of High Street, above what used to be called "The Island". This culm was dug out and used for making black paint. The works for its manufacture were at the top of Cold Harbour. Pitt Lane almost certainly got its name from these same culm pits, at the top of the hill.

Meddon Street is a corruption of Maiden Street which, in a lease of 1620, was spelt Mayden Street. Honestone Street in 1707 was known as Horestone Lane.

Following the cutting of the Rolle Canal, Bideford's New Torrington Road was constructed in 1827. The original plan was for the road to connect with Buttgarden Street up Torridge Hill; a level road from the bridge southwards was not even considered at the time. The tradespeople around the Market Place naturally preferred the top approach, and those

near the quay pressed for the lower. Eventually, both were constructed, the tradesmen at the bottom of the town helping to contribute to the construction of the New Road, as it is still called.

Nunnery Walk, behind Tanton's Hotel, is so called from a Nunnery which stood at the bottom of Lower Meddon Street, near Marine Gardens; the old door and cellars can still be seen.

Buttgarden Street was built near the town's Archery Butts, an archery shooting range.

Above: These houses, known as "The island", once stood at the top of Bideford High Street at the junction with Pitt Lane.

Top left: Lower Meddon street where the Church Institute now stands.

Bottom left: during the early years of the twentieth century the Church Army organised travelling soup kitchens like this one which operated in the Bideford area.

Little America, near the coach-drive, reached by the New Road, is thought to be a corruption of Littleham Mer (or mere), meaning marsh.

Before 1827, the only approach to Torrington was up Torrington Lane and via Gammaton, then along narrow country lanes.

Up to about 1880, all the streets of the neighbourhood were cobbled. At Appledore, the market was built in 1828, and was also cobbled. This fascinating village has lost none of its character, possibly due to the fact that it is at the end of the peninsula on which Bideford and district stands. It has never been a place for just "passing through", but stands in its own right. All around are fascinating signs of its being a village of seamen. When the old wooden sailing ships were broken up, good timbers were kept for building houses. It is not surprising to find trellis work in the garden supported by a taffrail.

Left and below: Neither the Appledore seaweed gatherers nor the boys were wearing shoes when these photographs were taken in 1904.

The street called Factory Ope, joining Appledore Quay, got its name from a malt factory, which gave way in 1878 to Duncan and Vincent's Collar Factory, an off-shoot from their works at Westcombe at Bideford.

Above: Appledore Quay at the beginning of the twentieth century.

Top right: Myrtle Street, Appledore, about 1910. The buildings seen here behind the cart were demolished in 1933 when the main road was driven through to the quay.

Bottom right: Irsha Street, Appledore, in 1910.

Binney's Slip about 1860

River and quay

The River Torridge used to be very much wider in the days before Bideford Quay was widened and the Pill enclosed. The water reached to the bottom of Raleigh Hill, the Causeway being covered except at low tide. On the east side of the river, the tide reached Pill Head. A favourite boat trip for Bidefordians before 1890 was said to be from Binney's (or Bunney's) Slip, just below where Tanton's Hotel now stands, around to Orchard Hill, which was then a gorse-covered meadow.

SHORTENED BIBLIOGRAPHY

The Devonshire Domesday

The Transactions of the Devonshire Association

The Gentleman's Magazine

Anglo-Saxon Chronicle, translated by GN Garmonsway, 1953.

Asser's Life of King Alfred, edited by WH Stevenson, 1904.

The History of Bideford, John Watkins, 1792.

Worthies of Devon, John Prince, 1810.

History and Directory of Devonshire, William White, 1850.

Survey of the County of Devon, Tristram Risdon, 1811.

Magna Britannia (Devonshire), Rev Daniel and Samuel Lysons,1822.

Bideford Directory, William White, 1850.

Principal Navigations, Richard Hakluyt, 1589.

The Silver Map of Drake's Voyage, Miller Christy.

The Industries of North Devon, HW Strong, 1881.

Barnstaple and the Northern Part of Devonshire During the Great Civil War, RW Cotton, 1889.

Devon, WG Hoskins, 1954.

Georgian England, AE Richardson, 1931.

The Saxon Conquest of Somerset and Devon, HM Porter, 1967.

Westcountrymen in Prince Edward's Island, Basil Greenhill, 1967.

OLD BIDEFORD AND DISTRICT

INDEX

Page numbers in italics refer to illustrations

OLD BIDEFORD AND DISTRICT